KRYSTAL HIGG

BETTER
ONBOARDING

Publisher: Krystal Higgins

Managing editor: Lisa Maria Marquis
Editors: Sally Kerrigan, Caren Litherland,
        Danielle Small, Christopher Hagge
Book producer: Ron Bilodeau

*This title was originally published by A Book
        Apart and has been republished by the
        author. Thank you to the A Book Apart
        team who first brought the book to life:
        Jeffrey Zeldman, Jason Santa Maria, and
        Katel LeDû.*

ISBN: 978-1-7636734-0-3

TABLE OF CONTENTS

To Christine,
for always being there,
no matter the distance

FOREWORD

IN MY TWELVE-PLUS YEARS as a design leader, I have spent countless hours trying to determine how to make new employees' first weeks on the job both educational and engaging. How can I best set them up for success and introduce them to the team? Documentation? Videos? A buddy system?

These are the same kinds of questions that designers should ask about new users. How can we introduce them to our products in a way that's both educational and engaging—*and* keeps them coming back? User onboarding is the quintessential first step of their journey, but it's a step too often sidelined, rushed, or ignored in the overall product strategy.

Fortunately for us, Krystal Higgins has spent years studying onboarding experiences in product design, and is ready to share the tried-and-true principles and frameworks that truly speak to (and retain) new users. Krystal addresses the macro and micro questions of guided interaction, from "Why bother with onboarding?" to "Should I use a tutorial?" (spoiler: no). Above all, she understands the tough work of aligning teams and helping them avoid common onboarding pitfalls.

The biggest pitfall of all might be our own preconceived notions of what makes a good onboarding experience. Krystal rightly dismantles the myth that user onboarding is a one-and-done activity, focusing instead on long-term interactions. As someone who is passionate about designing for growth in a customer-centric way, I was delighted to find that this book treats onboarding as a holistic part of the product experience, not as a single business metric.

I invite you to unlearn the onboarding mistakes of the past, and immerse yourself in this comprehensive, scientific, and actionable roadmap to guided interaction. Onboarding is your first impression with your customer. Don't make it the last!

—Chetana Deorah

"LET'S GET STARTED!"

MY FIRST TECH ROLE was at a company that specialized in printers and copiers, and I was responsible for designing their setup flows. I had studied narrative animation and illustration, so I approached the setup flows like a story: a narrative for onboarding new users to the features and functionality of the company's devices. I plotted and illustrated a step-by-step sequence of screens, bookending them with nice-looking covers—a "Let's get started!" screen at the beginning, and a "You're all set!" success screen at the end.

But I quickly learned I couldn't rely on that approach. I couldn't plot out the path users would take to set up their printers, and I couldn't guarantee they'd arrive at the ending I'd had in mind because people act in all sorts of different ways for all sorts of different reasons. I also didn't think about the post-setup support that people would need after they'd tossed aside their user manual or sped through setup, or whether the person setting up the printer would even *be* the person using it every day.

I wasn't alone in my instinct to treat onboarding as a story; I'm sure you've seen your fair share of products that kick off with "Let's get started!" and end with "You're all set!" As designers, we're often taught that narrative is the answer to whatever problem we're trying to solve. And stories are indeed very useful, especially when helping your team build and market products.

But new users haven't come to hear the story of your product—they want to get things done. If we treat products like a story to be told, we'll be disappointed when they fail to follow the plot we've laid out for them. A core tenet of interaction design is that experiences should be driven by the people who use them, yet a narrative approach isn't user-centered—it's inherently product-centered. We need a better method for onboarding and guiding users.

Does your product need a better approach to onboarding?

Product teams spend so much time and money attracting new users to their products, yet struggle to retain those users because they don't have a strategy for guiding them over time. Front-loaded instructions fail to help people personally connect with the experience and fail to capture their initial interest in trying something new. Products need to support new users coming from different situations, and single-sized explanations don't cut it. And, with products becoming increasingly intelligent and personalized, it's just plain difficult to predict and explain up front what kind of experience a new user will have.

How can you tell if your product's existing approach to onboarding needs work? Look for these signs:

- You have lower retention or engagement numbers compared to other similar products—and users who get hands-on, in-person help during their first thirty to sixty days are more successful than those who receive a lesser level of support. This indicates your overall product value may be strong, but you're not supporting new users in a way that helps them realize that.
- Your team spends a lot of time maintaining tutorials, setup flows, and slideshows because they're frequently out of date. While onboarding experiences require maintenance just like any good product experience, if you find yourself spending too much money and energy updating static content in the same place over and over again, it may mean you're missing out on better investments at other points in the experience.
- A high number of users abandon or skip existing tutorials and other types of educational content. If you're using these formats as your primary means for guiding users, then those high dismissal rates mean users aren't getting much guidance at all.
- Existing users report being confused by current product behaviors that resulted from decisions they made. If new users don't understand the decisions they're making when

setting up something new, unpleasant surprises can pop up, like suddenly receiving a large number of unexpected notifications.

- You have a high volume of customer support requests from new folks during their first thirty to sixty days, despite those issues supposedly being addressed by your current onboarding solution. While *no* onboarding experience can guarantee users won't contact customer support, a significant number of tickets can indicate you need better guidance.

A sound approach to user onboarding will set up your product to:

- support wide audiences,
- increase retention and engagement,
- decrease customer service costs,
- reduce difficult-to-maintain standalone flows, and
- introduce changes and new additions over time.

A better path forward

The best onboarding experiences guide people as they interact, instead of explaining things in narrative form. Together, we will cover how to use guided interaction rather than linear storytelling to help users follow their own path to success. And, yes, while this book is presented in a narrative manner, it will provide you with practical, hands-on strategies for designing effective guidance. The techniques found here are just as applicable to guiding users through product redesigns, new-feature introductions, service updates, and returns after a lapse as they are for the initial onboarding of new users.

I don't expect you will diligently read through the contents of this book before you even start working on user onboarding. You might be just starting a new onboarding project, in the middle of designing an onboarding experience, or still trying to convince your team—and even yourself—why you should invest in one. My hope is that the different sections of this book will serve as a helpful guide no matter where you are in your design process.

The advice that follows has been gleaned from my own experiences working as an in-house designer on various teams across various products; borrowed from the literature and works of others in the fields of UX, HR, games, and more; and shaped by the perspectives of those I've been honored to facilitate and chat with in workshops, discussions, and other environments. Now it's my turn to pass it along to you. Let's get started.

1

WHAT IS ONBOARDING?

I USED TO WORK ON SMARTWATCHES at a time when consumers considered them fairly novel. The teams I worked with were interested in helping people see the value of wearing a smartwatch by teaching them how to use it to enhance their daily lives. These devices were prime candidates for a good onboarding experience.

Eventually, I joined the Android Wear (now Wear OS by Google) team to help them with the setup and onboarding design of their smartwatch experience. At the time, the team had just received a round of feedback that some customers weren't aware of all the features of their new watch, which could lead to inconsistent use. The team had just kicked off work on a tutorial video meant to appear on the phone app used to set up a new watch.

The theory behind adding this video was reasonable: because setup required the smartwatch to be connected to a mobile phone app, users could watch a how-to video on their phone while they waited for the watch to finish the setup process. The end product was a lovely, ninety-second animated video that highlighted key features of the watch (**FIG 1.1**).

FIG 1.1: An early version of the Wear OS by Google mobile app showed a video to new watch owners while they were setting up their watches.

FIG 1.2: Subsequent versions of the Wear OS by Google smartwatch experience included more on-watch interactive guidance, such as sample notifications that provided contextual tips.

However, we found that the video had few views, and participants in research studies often skipped it. The video's instructional nature and linear formatting forced the viewer into a passive state, but they had just unboxed a new watch and were interested in trying it out! So, they ignored it, or skipped it, so they could start playing with their watch. Those who did view the video didn't demonstrate any deeper comprehension of how the watch functioned than those who hadn't.

Ultimately, the combination of user research results, a low view count, and the work involved in making updates to the video every time the watch interface changed convinced the team to remove the video from the setup experience. When the effort expended on keeping the video up-to-date was compared to the limited benefit of the video on onboarding end-users, it became clear that it should go.

Now, the video wasn't the only thing the team had included to help acclimate new users. The watch also offered interactive, optional on-watch educational tips that users could move through at their own pace (**FIG 1.2**). This was an interactive technique the team iterated and expanded on in future releases. And videos? They found a different use—in a prepurchase capacity, often shown alongside demo devices at stores.

This example shows how you can remove a piece of front-loaded instruction and focus instead on guidance in the context of direct interaction. As we'll see in the next section, the latter is a more effective approach to user onboarding.

ONBOARDING IS A JOURNEY

We have a tendency to think of user onboarding as a single moment of orientation, after which your new users will be operating on all cylinders. Perhaps that's because many of us encounter the term in the context of joining a new company, where the word gets used to describe a series of presentations, videos, building tours, introductions...and the completion of lots and lots of forms. It's this orientation-focused perception that has us holding firm to the notion that product onboarding can be solved with a one-size-fits-all piece of introductory content.

But onboarding *isn't* a single moment, or a single feature, or a single flow. It's a process that connects many activities, over time, to bridge the gap between trying a new product and becoming a core user of it. Tutorials, videos, setup flows, slideshows, and signup flows may all be a *part* of that journey, but none alone *are* the journey.

Effective onboarding handles multiple jobs that lead to retention, engagement, and commitment of newcomers to our products by:

- building trust,
- familiarizing them with a product's offerings,
- setting up logistics,
- leading them to making a commitment, and
- guiding them toward next steps until they achieve a steady state.

Given this scope, onboarding needs more than one moment of orientation to do all its work. In the employment world, companies have been expanding the time frame for *employee* onboarding programs because those that are six to twelve

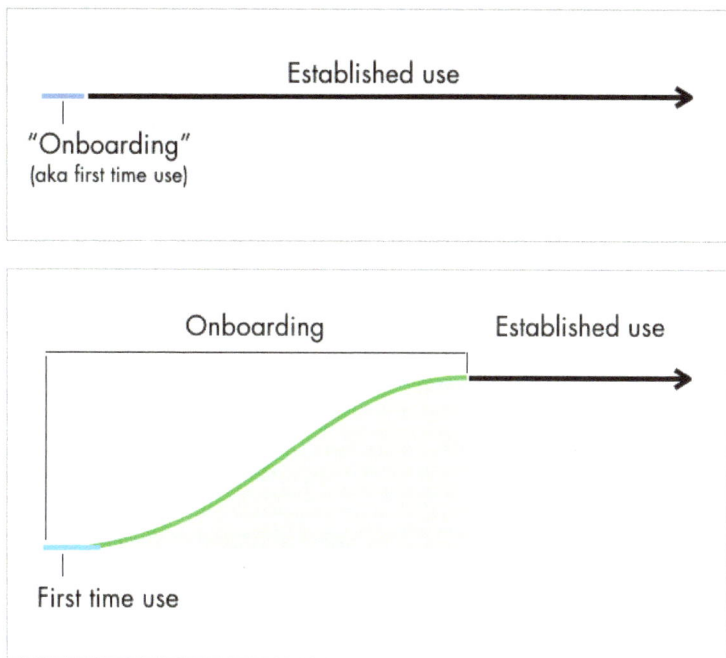

FIG 1.3: When we design onboarding, we often only think about the first-time use of our product and expect all issues to be sorted out afterward (top). But onboarding is a process that happens over time, guiding nascent users toward commitment and satisfaction (bottom).

months long better support employee retention, loyalty, performance, and job satisfaction [1]. In the product world, we don't necessarily have to view onboarding as a six- to twelve-month process, but we do have to think beyond day one if we want to help users in their most critical stages of acclimation (**FIG 1.3**).

Viewing onboarding as a process over time doesn't diminish the importance of making a good first impression on day one. Many teams focus on creating a good first impression, which inspires users to keep going and sets them up for continued success. A bad first impression can cause users to leave a product prematurely, or predisposes them to think negatively about their future interactions [2]. Sometimes, though, we get so caught up in that first impression that we ignore what follows.

It's *because* the first impression is so important that we can't think of onboarding only as a one-time event. If we hold that mindset, we end up with a first impression that's stuffed full of all the information and tasks we want a new user to get through, instead of something that builds interest and excitement, leaving nothing to help that person immediately afterward. Though a good first impression gives new users initial momentum, they'll need additional support to get them into a steady state.

There's one question I've heard many variations of throughout my career, and chances are you've heard it, too: "New users aren't discovering all of our features," someone will say. "Can't we show them a video or tour to make sure they know about everything?" This gets asked when we notice people aren't using our product the way we envisioned. We see data that shows poor engagement with the features we've built, we hear customers bemoan lack of functionality that already exists, or we watch participants struggle during a usability test. An instructional video or tour presented at the beginning of an experience should ensure everyone knows how to use our product's features, right? Who are we to say no to such a reasonable-sounding request?

Yet, passive instructional techniques like videos, tutorials, and slideshows often fail to onboard newcomers effectively. But why? Enter a concept known as the *paradox of the active user*, first named by Mary Beth Rosson and John M. Carroll, researchers at IBM in the 1980s [3]. Rosson and Carroll were studying how people acclimated to computer software. They noticed participants in their studies seldom referred to the training guides provided to them, and instead dived right into new software to try a few tasks for themselves. They did this even if it meant encountering errors and dead ends.

How come? Because the new users were motivated by the specific goals they wanted to achieve, not by the larger potential of the technology. They were uninterested in taking time up front to learn about all the features they *might* benefit from in the future when there were actions they could *definitely* benefit from immediately. As a result, each person's understanding of what this software was capable of was often limited to the tasks they did first. Rosson and Carroll called this a paradox because people could get more from software if they spent time learning about it up front. However, we can't design for this because people don't behave in such an idealized way.

THE PERILS OF FRONT-LOADED INSTRUCTION

You might not think such troubles apply to your app or website. After all, how many digital products these days even have a user manual? But these printed behemoths have simply evolved into other forms for the digital space: video tours, explanatory slideshows, lengthy informational pages, UI mapping overlays, popups, and more—all trying to explain our products up front instead of letting people simply dive in (**FIG 1.4**).

It's tempting to think that today's users will be so motivated by the larger promise of our products that they'll eagerly sit through front-loaded instruction. But that's not how most people actually behave.

Using front-loaded instruction as a strategy for solving user onboarding is problematic for a few reasons:

- **It tries to predict the future.** Front-loaded instruction tries to tell people about what they need, based on what a product team thinks they need to hear. But people come to our products from different contexts, and we can't predict what they'll actually care about.
- **It's hard to remember.** When we rely on putting all our instructions up front, people only have one chance to memorize it. Unfortunately, people tend to forget things they only encounter a single time.
- **It's overwhelming**. In a chapter called "Designing Organizations for an Information-Rich World" in *Computers, Communications, and the Public Interest*, social scientist Herbert A. Simon noted that "a wealth of information creates a poverty of attention." A person's short-term memory has limited capacity, and presenting all information at once will

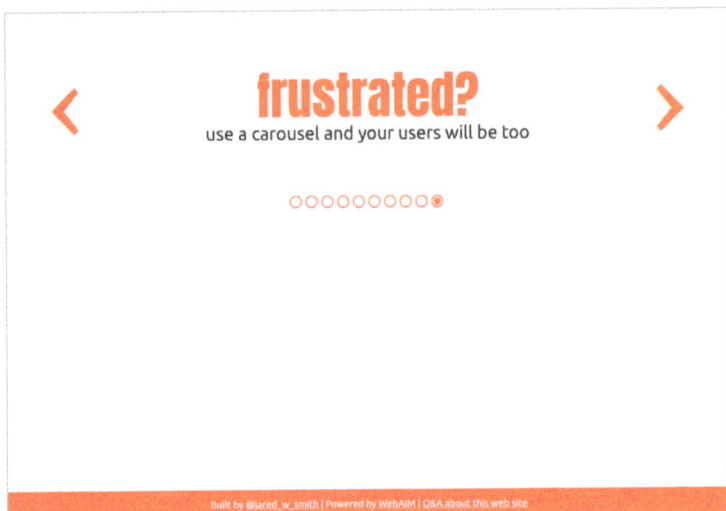

frustrated?
use a carousel and your users will be too

○○○○○○○○○◉

FIG 1.4: Jared Smith created shouldiuseacarousel.com as a tongue-in-cheek illustration of how front-loaded explanatory patterns like carousels and slideshows are ineffective.

result in only a portion—if any at all—of that information being remembered.

- **It can make a product seem overly complex.** Taking time during a user's first use of a product to explain or introduce features can make the product seem more complicated than it really is. In a 2020 usability test, Nielsen Norman Group found that users who sat through a product tutorial rated the concepts taught by it as more difficult than did users who skipped the tutorial [4].

- **It's a lot of work to maintain and scale.** Tutorials, videos, or other explanatory content rely on taking a snapshot of how a product exists at a given time. Whenever something changes, you need to republish the content, or risk new users being greeted with outdated material. Did you add support for new countries? If so, now you need to localize that introductory content, which can mean re-rendering videos, visuals, or audio. Did you remove, redesign, or add a key feature? Now you must perform surgery on your introductory content to change the relevant bits.

- **It's out of context.** Presenting introductory tours, slide-shows, or tutorials up front makes it harder for people to really understand and apply the content because it's presented out of context and ahead of a product they haven't even tried yet.
- **It's focused on awareness, not follow-through.** When we onboard new users, we're often trying to encourage new behaviors, whether that's trying to get a user to move from one solution to ours, to do a task in a new way, or to do a new kind of task altogether. Yet simply raising awareness of our offerings and functionality doesn't guarantee action. In "Stop Raising Awareness Already," authors Ann Christiano and Annie Neimand warn that focusing on raising awareness, instead of developing deeper strategies that drive behavior change through meaningful action, leads to subpar results [5].

THE PERILS OF UNSUPPORTED IMMERSION

Do the risks of relying on front-loaded instruction mean that we should instead launch newcomers into our full product experience, unaided? Not exactly. Just as we can't force people to "read the manual" before they can get immersed in something unfamiliar, we can't drop every new person into the deep end of our product and assume they'll be successful. Unsupported immersion comes with its own problems:

- **It can also overwhelm.** In the same way that presenting too many choices up front as part of an explicit setup flow or tutorial might be overwhelming, dropping a new user into a product without any guidance as to what to do first can also be overwhelming and disheartening.
- **It can exclude audiences.** Game designer Carol Mertz noted that many game designers "want" players who can figure out their game without help [6]. This problematic attitude ends up restricting the audience that can actually play the game.

Similarly, we can fall into the trap of assuming that our product is so "simple" that anyone should be able to figure it out. But researchers working on the GenderMag project have found there are many different approaches to learning new technologies—some users are willing to take on more risk and tinker around, while others are more risk-averse and want to take a more comprehensive approach [7].

The audiences you want to bring into your product as new users include both people who are familiar with an experience like yours, and those who are less familiar with it. You need an approach that figures out the happy medium between providing support to new users and offering flexibility for those who want to just jump in.

A BETTER WAY FORWARD

To effectively onboard new users, we can't rely on all of them to read or watch a video about our features, settings, and UI right away and expect them to be successful when they're in the thick of things. And we can't drop them into a new space without any support. So what should we do?

It turns out that classroom educators have explored this problem. Educational researcher Roxana Moreno and educational psychologist Richard Mayer studied how teaching environments could most effectively help students learn new concepts. They found that students learned better when these environments interactively guided someone throughout their lessons instead of relying on passive information or letting the students engage in pure discovery [8].

While we shouldn't get too wrapped up in the idea that our products are equivalent to classroom spaces (people typically don't come to sites or apps expecting a lesson!), this is a concept that easily applies to digital products. Game developer George Fan cites this kind of balance for teaching people to play video games: ideally, guidance blends seamlessly into standard gameplay, so that you might never know you were guided through a tutorial at all. He used this strategy in the game *Plants vs.*

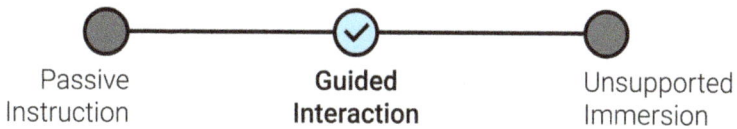

Passive Instruction — Guided Interaction — Unsupported Immersion

FIG 1.5: Guided interaction is the happy medium between front-loaded instruction and unsupported immersion.

Zombies 2, where the first level used simple challenges to familiarize players with key components of gameplay before taking on more complex levels. For Fan, it's a compliment if a player says they didn't notice the game had a tutorial, but he posits that there's a difference between a game not having a *memorable* tutorial and one not having *any* support [9].

Research and case studies have showed us we can't lecture our new users up front with passive instruction, but we also can't cast them adrift, leaving them to sort everything out themselves. Instead, we need to weave guidance into the key interactions of our products so new users can immerse themselves in our experience, and have the support they need to be successful. I call this approach *guided interaction* (**FIG 1.5**).

Guided interaction helps users understand a product more than an approach that relies only on explaining the product up front. Whether it's starting a new routine or learning to ride a bike, integrating almost anything new into our lives involves learning-through-doing. Participating directly in an activity is a more effective way for us to grasp its mechanics and how it can be adjusted to fit our individual needs over time [10]. As an onboarding design strategy, guided interaction embraces this idea, leveraging the excitement of jumping into something new as a foundation for support.

This is about more than just onboarding for onboarding's sake. When we guide via interaction, we're being deliberate. Here's what this involves:

- We connect the information to the meaningful actions that education enables, instead of explaining things out of context.

- We decouple the important actions of our onboarding experience so new users in different situations can encounter them at the time and in the order that suits them, using guidance to lead to next steps that build toward a long-term goal.
- We use types of guidance that are an authentic extension of our baseline product experience, instead of something tacked on or disruptive.

Now, the idea of relying on guided interaction can be worrisome for some teams. Both front-loaded instruction and unsupported immersion are strategies born of a fear of risk. Fear that customers might have a negative experience because of missteps or missed information can lead teams to skew toward front-loaded instruction. Other teams fear the friction of adding guidance to their experience because they equate "number of clicks" or additional structure with whether an experience is good or not. Indeed, unnecessary work put on the user can lead to abandonment. But effective guidance isn't about total lack of effort. You're building an onboarding experience that embraces a *meaningful* effort that helps people understand how their use of your products, services, and technologies fit into their lives.

INTERACT, DON'T TELL

Instead of trying to show or tell new users how to proceed through their onboarding journey with a single, one-time flow, we are better off using guided interaction to support them as they move through the steps.

How does guided interaction manifest itself, then? Back to the earlier Wear OS by Google smartwatch example: after the instructional video was removed, the product's approach to onboarding new users reflected a more contextual, gradual approach.

- The setup flow focused on getting the user to only turn on features needed for the watch to get to a ready state.
- Once the watch was ready to use, placeholder notifications (which had been unobtrusively added to the watch right

FIG 1.6: When users activated the Google Assistant for the first time on an earlier version of Wear OS by Google, they were greeted by a contextual set of suggestions.

as setup was completed) let people try out different interactions and flick through examples of how future content would appear—at their own pace.

- And, as users progressed through different sections of the watch, they received additional hints. For instance, once someone opened the Google Assistant for the first time, they were shown a first-time message with examples of what they could say to it (**FIG 1.6**).
- That's just *one* example of how guided interaction might play out, but the way it will surface for different products will—and should—be different. The rest of this book will help you figure out what's right for your product.

It's time to dive into what it takes to design a good onboarding experience using guided interaction. But before we can break down and tackle the work of the onboarding experience, let's look at some of the things we need to do internally to get ready for new users.

2 GETTING READY FOR NEW USERS

ONCE, WHEN WORKING ON A CONSUMER WEBSITE, I asked why we prompted new visitors to agree to an end user license agreement (EULA) up front. One colleague responded that the practice helped users because if they accepted the EULA at the outset, they wouldn't have to deal with it later on. You might not be able to get around showing an end user license agreement, but "getting stuff out of the way" is certainly not an effective mindset to have when guiding your new users.

I never really knew if this was the *actual* reason it was done this way (I expect and hope it was more nuanced than that!), but it wouldn't surprise me if it were. Unfortunately, these misguided decisions are often side effects of a user onboarding experience built as an afterthought, without the right pieces in place.

Guided interaction, the process of guiding users *as* they use your product, requires a more thoughtful, integrated approach. A fair number of the challenges I have experienced (and still experience) in user onboarding have stemmed from unclear or misguided goals that the team should have been aligned on before the project kicked off.

A team may be kicking off an onboarding experience for any number of reasons. Maybe you're in the process of pitching your team or stakeholders to invest in redoing yours. Maybe you have a new product and know you'll need to guide new users into it. Or perhaps your team has already been tasked with revising an onboarding experience and is raring to jump in and go.

But before you can dive into the nitty-gritty of bringing guided interaction to life, it's helpful to get your team and product ready to welcome new users. This involves:

- aligning your team,
- building a new user mindset, and
- clearing first-impression roadblocks.

ALIGNING YOUR TEAM

When you're designing onboarding, you'll be working with a number of cross-functional stakeholders, such as UX professionals, product managers, user researchers, engineers, and others responsible for the day-to-day process of building a product. You'll likely also be interacting with a few managers or executives that make or approve product decisions.

Each of these roles may view onboarding in different ways that affect how and if onboarding work is allocated:

- "We shouldn't need onboarding; the product speaks for itself!"
- "Onboarding work is competing with other feature work."
- "We should use the same onboarding patterns our competitors use."
- "Let's just use a premade onboarding widget, so that we don't have to build our own."

Differing opinions on how to approach onboarding design often stem from different goals. You'll create a much better onboarding experience for your new users if your team is aligned on the right goals.

Avoid using short-term measures in isolation

A front-loaded, one-and-done instructional experience can often be the result of a team focusing too much on addressing short-term metrics. Acquisition—the number of new people brought into an experience—is commonly used as a proxy for onboarding success. It's often measured in terms of number of accounts created, free trials started, unique visitors to a website, or app installations. Sometimes, product teams will measure completion rates of setup flows or tutorials to determine if they're successful or not. Analytics tools have sprung up *en masse* to make these short-term outcomes easy to measure, perpetuating their adoption.

While short-term metrics like completion rate, free trials started, and app installs can measure the reach of your marketing channels or the optimization of your signup flow, they aren't reliable indicators that new users will stick around. They're often called *vanity metrics* because they're superficial measures that don't represent the bigger picture of product health and onboarding success.

Optimizing for vanity metrics can hurt us in the long term. A product might push new users to sign up right away to drive up acquisition numbers, but see a drop in overall retention because the ask is more than people are willing to commit to. Consider this cautionary tale: In 2010, the *Times*, a *Guardian* property, switched to a mandatory request for visitors to sign up for an account, and reportedly lost 90 percent of its readership as a result of that shift [1]. Be mindful about optimizing for vanity metrics in the larger context of your longer-term product goals.

Connect to longer-term goals

After hearing all of this, you may be tempted to have your organization set "design user onboarding" as an explicit strategic goal so your team takes it seriously. But this approach can backfire just as much as a goal focused on vanity metrics, unless all parties understand how user onboarding manifests. If they don't, odds are they'll reduce it to a single, front-loaded flow to show quick accomplishment of that goal...and you'll end up back down the path of optimizing for short-term metrics.

It's important to realize onboarding works toward the same goals we have for our products as a whole: to help users succeed, and to reach a state where their successes advance our organization's business goals. This means onboarding design efforts should be focused on improving retention (how many people stick around to use the product over days, weeks, or months) and engagement (the extent to which they use the product's key features). According to one study, customers who reported having a good onboarding experience were more likely to pay for a subscription than those who didn't [2].

You can also hitch your product's onboarding experience to existing organizational goals. For example, if your company has a goal to scale to a new audience, you might share how revisiting the way guidance is applied in your current onboarding experience can improve the ability to retain new audiences and make "improved onboarding experience" a step toward achieving that goal.

It's okay to use short-term metrics that measure acquisition or conversion, but to gauge the health of your onboarding experience, they should be analyzed alongside overall retention or engagement. A high number of signups paired with low retention tells a different story than a high number of signups paired with high retention.

That also goes for feedback from usability studies conducted on a single flow. Testing how someone completes an individual signup flow or tutorial only gives you a short-term lens. You may discover understandability issues in a focused study session, but it's also possible for someone to breeze through one flow only to experience issues later on. Any findings should be put into the larger context of studying long-term comprehension and measuring retention and engagement.

Align with the extended team

Aligning on a shared goal for user onboarding doesn't need to stop with your primary working partners and stakeholders. There are other product professionals, perhaps in other organizations at your company, who can influence what newcomers get out of user onboarding. Make sure you pull them into the process of designing onboarding and that they understand and share the goals you've set for that experience. By bringing these professionals into the mix, you can greatly improve support for new users. When the following people *aren't* part of the process, are brought in too late, or aren't aligned to the same goals as the rest of your team, you can end up with a journey that falls flat, or sudden constraints that you have to rush to incorporate.

- **Copywriters** can be beneficial in their ability to help you craft words and set a tone that best helps newcomers relate to a new product or service.
- **Quality assurance (QA) professionals** test new user flows and find the bugs or issues that need to be solved to create a better experience. Helping these professionals understand the goals of your onboarding experience, and how it should behave, can help them write accurate test cases and give meaningful and contextual feedback.
- **Marketing** sets expectations before users come to our products, and those expectations need to map to what the product ends up delivering. Strategies for acquiring new users is not the focus of this book, but I encourage you to think about the situations in which people enter our products, and how those scenarios influence the onboarding experience.
- **Customer service professionals** may be the first to hear about new-user pain points and questions. They can help you understand any limitations of relying on customer service to solve problems for new users, and can be a consistent resource of feedback from real users of your product. In turn, letting customer service professionals know you're redesigning an experience for new users, and what it will involve, can better prepare them for the kinds of questions and issues those new users might encounter.
- **Legal, privacy, security, and other compliance teams** establish requirements that may result in opt-ins, notices, and other material changes to your onboarding experience. By working alongside these teams and understanding relevant requirements, you might be able to get ahead of future

requirements and to understand the scope of what you can and can't do before you invest too heavily in a solution. No team enjoys having a late-stage screen added to their to-do list because of a failure to identify these kinds of requirements up front.

Including these folks in your design process can help prevent surprise requirements—and might even result in having new champions to help you make your case.

BUILDING A NEW USER MINDSET

Knowledge about user goals, interests, and needs forms the basis of *any* interaction design, and that's doubly true when thinking about how your product approaches incoming users. Sometimes we lose focus on new users as we start listening to more and more existing users through our research, customer support forums, and review sites. When we do that, we might make risky assumptions that prevent us from welcoming our products' new users.

I experienced this kind of assumption gut-check when I worked on a professional web tool. I wasn't planning on surfacing any kind of tutorial content in the first-run flows because our existing users never used them. But when the team researcher interviewed some of these users, they expressed less confidence in professional tools that didn't offer some kind of tutorial content in the first-run flow. It turns out this wasn't a matter of these professionals frequently using tutorial content, but because they had grown so accustomed to *other* tools having tutorials, they took this content as a signal that a product was serious about supporting them. I made sure to include a link to our customer service guides on one of the early screens of our product to reassure them that such content was available.

It's important to check your assumptions about new users with research that can help you understand what they expect, and why.

Incorporating new users into research

I suggest recruiting new users into existing research you have planned, when possible, and not just limiting their recruitment to research specifically for new-user onboarding. You can even occasionally pull from audiences that you may scale to (but haven't yet) as these will give you fresh perspectives to keep in mind for the future.

The following kinds of questions are just some of the things you can incorporate into the research you're already doing:

- **How and why did they find your product?** Are they being directed from web search links, advertisements, referrals from friends, or other sources? Are they looking to switch from another product, or is yours the first they've used?
- **What are their expectations?** What products or similar concepts have new users engaged with that might influence their thought process? What kinds of assumptions do they have?
- **How have they approached trying other new products?** Understanding the different methods people might use when trying your product can help you understand how they might tackle yours.
- **What's worked or hasn't worked with other new products?** Understanding the barriers that people have encountered in other products can help you to convince your team to remove or prevent barriers from existing in yours.
- **What common routines do established users lean on in and outside of your product that new users need to be guided to doing?** Understanding the different ways your established users have sustained their success can help you determine how to guide new users.
- **What workarounds have your existing users developed?** Seeing the kinds of hacks your steadfast, existing users have developed can help you understand what you'll need to address for new users.

If your product research includes new users, you will likely learn about ways your core product can improve. Often, implementing those core product changes can lead to a better user onboarding experience. Even if you know your team doesn't have the bandwidth to make overall product changes in the short term, keep track of these findings.

And even if you're not currently running foundational research with new users, you can learn from them in the day-to-day testing of your existing product. Recruit a few new users into the usability studies you've already planned. You might need to ask them different questions, but running research with both new and existing users simultaneously can really clarify the gaps between their understanding.

Keeping the new-user mindset fresh in your team

People working day-to-day on a product's details can lose sight of what a new user experiences. Counteract this by immersing your team in the mindset of new users as much as possible. Talking to potential new users will help, but there are many ways to extend and maintain this mindset within your team:

- **Set up multiple channels for people to access insights about new users.** Invite colleagues to observe research sessions. Enable your teammates to shadow customer service calls or view anonymized customer service chat transcripts. Set up a system for your team to keep regular tabs on user research and onboarding feedback, such as a shared document or a dedicated channel using Slack collaboration software.
- **Ask teammates to journal their onboarding experiences with other products.** Paying attention to and sharing first-time experiences should be an ongoing touchpoint. Rotate team members through a list of assigned projects or have lunch sessions where they share a recent experience. Ask new hires to spend their first week or month journaling their experience with *your* product before they become embedded in the company mindset. This isn't a substitute for user research, but it can remind the team about what it's like to try something new.

- **Explore your product in "new user mode."** Ensure that everyone on your team can access your product in exactly the same way that new users do. For apps, wipe any local data, account data, and system permissions from the app, and clear any stored system permissions granted from the device it's running on. Use a private browsing mode for web products, which will often clear stored user information. For devices, reset them to their factory default settings to get back to the setup experience all new users face. If your product involves creating an account or paying for a subscription, set up test accounts to understand the initial flows new users encounter as they sign up for your product.
- **Roleplay your new user experience as a team.** This will build a visceral understanding of the frustrations or confusions new users might encounter. Ask a colleague to play the role of the product, and another to play the role of the new user, with the rest of your team as audience. Set up a device to run as a new user would experience it, or display mockups or screenshots of your onboarding experience. Then, the person playing the role of the product will narrate or act out what they see, and the person playing the role of the user will react by articulating their thoughts or taking an action. It's a fun ad-lib experience, but you'll quickly see if you're welcoming, frustrating, or confusing new users. You can get a template of this structured approach for scripting and playing out this activity on my website at www.kryshiggins. com/coach.

Balancing new and existing users

While some teams gravitate to the needs of existing users because they're simply more available, others can over-index on new users because they're easier to recruit—for most products, there are more people who *haven't* used your experience than have. You don't want to overdesign your product's experience for new users in a way that treats existing ones like newbies. It's critical to balance the experience for both new and existing users.

Separating new users from those who have already been onboarded is, unfortunately, only a partially solved problem. There are several technical approaches that might help you identify the difference between the two, but each has caveats:

- **Local storage.** For most software installed on a device, you can tell if someone is using it for the first, second, or n number of times by storing information about their prior activities locally. But that information can't tell you if that person has simply reinstalled the app or used it on another platform.
- **Cookies.** On a website, you can use cookies to understand (at least some of) a user's prior activities. However, use of tracking cookies does require user permission, and is governed by regulations that vary from region to region. And cookies can't provide helpful information if the user is browsing from a different device or in private browsing mode.
- **Accounts.** If a user sets up an account with your product, you can more easily keep track of their status and actions regardless of device or browsing context. But that can only tell you about the users who have signed up for an account, and you can't guarantee at which point in an experience each user will choose to do that. A given user might be faster or slower to create accounts than you anticipated, so it's harder to tell which users are truly new and which are returning.

Your ability to understand where in the onboarding experience someone is at a given time, and how much you are willing to risk being wrong, will later define how strongly you can push special guidance for new users. You'll still—as a designer and as a team—have to decide how you'll strike a balance between existing and new users. Luckily, guided interaction is predicated on the idea that we can weave guidance into the flow of our products, instead of lumping it all together up front or tacking it on superficially.

MAKING A GREAT FIRST IMPRESSION

Have you ever been eager to use something you just purchased only to realize it's sealed in terrible packaging you can only open after struggling for fifteen minutes with scissors and suffering a few cuts on your hand?

Now imagine having a frustrating experience like that, but with an easy-to-delete digital app. With the physical product, you might keep going because it's a hassle to return for no other reason than bad packaging. But with a digital product, it's oh-so-easy to get that nonsense out of your life.

Before you can expect a bunch of new users to enjoy your product, you need to make sure it is free from significant, obvious roadblocks that might stop a new user in their tracks. A good first impression, as we discussed in the previous chapter, is the key to getting new users in the door—but plenty of issues can get in the way, no matter how good of an onboarding experience you build:

- poor performance and reliability
- signup walls
- lack of inclusion
- hidden or unclear missions
  Let's look at how we can clear each of these roadblocks.

Poor performance and reliability

A good first impression is propped up by reliable products. They tell a new user: "You can trust that this product is secure, worth your time, and won't be a negative experience." The first run and onboarding flows of a product must load quickly, respond to interaction quickly, and be free of bugs.

Performance, especially, has a measurable effect on new user retention. Poor performance can cause people to abandon your experience, and it can lock out audiences that have internet speed or mobile data constraints [3]. In 2016, the *Financial Times* ran an experiment on their website by increasing its page-load time by one second every day. As a result, the rate of site abandonment went up, and the effect seemed to be greater for users who weren't previously highly engaged—suggesting that poor performance caused more new users, rather than existing users, to abandon the product [4]. A great onboarding experience after a long page-load time won't matter if there are no new users left to find it.

You also want to make sure your first-run experience is clear of bugs that disrupt the experience. A good example of such an issue is layout "jank," where content loaded incrementally causes elements on the page to jump around or pop up unpredictably. "At best, [jank] causes you to lose your place while reading; at worst, it can mean clicking on something you really didn't mean to," designer Chris Coyier wrote [5]. Review your site in its new-user mode to find potential jank and make the experience more reliable.

Signup walls

Many products push signup walls in front of new users, forcing people to make a commitment to the product before they can use any part of it. But, while some ubiquitous products *might* be justified in asking for this up front, most products don't have the luxury of wide scale recognition and clout. Just because someone has navigated to your website or downloaded your app doesn't mean they intended to commit to it!

As we read earlier in this chapter, forcing signup too early can cause new users to abandon our product, hurting long-term metrics like retention. In other cases, forced signup can lead to a proliferation of fake accounts if visitors choose to create accounts using false information. For example, a sample of UK consumers said they'd registered for accounts using fake information, partially because they felt the information asked of them was unnecessary so early on in their experience [6]. So even if you get a large number of users to sign up by forcing them to do so up front, there's no guarantee those accounts represent genuine, committed users. And, if that's the case, what's the point of asking?

Finally, putting signup walls in front of new users also means any arduous security requirements that underpin your signup

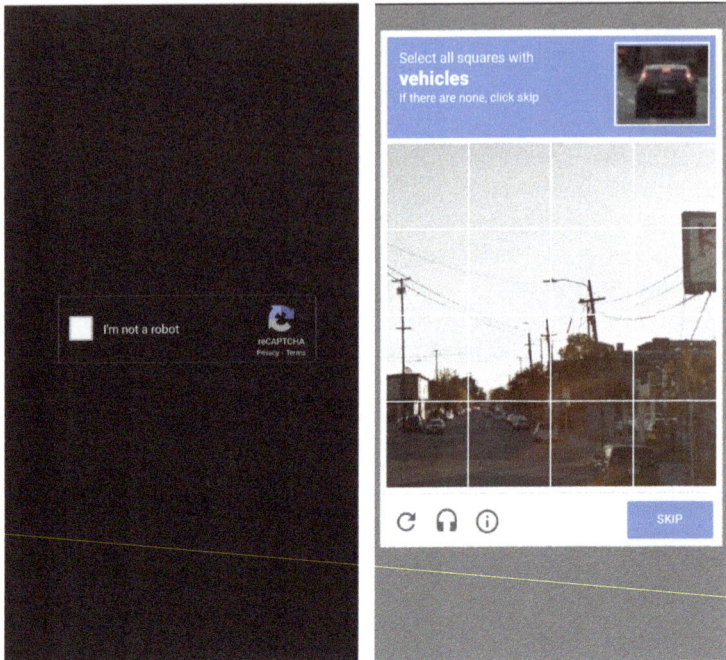

FIG 2.1: I recently signed up for a service that forced me to create an account up front. After providing login information, I was immediately pushed into a CAPTCHA experience that required three separate image confirmations before I could effectively save my account.

flow become front and center as a new user forms their first impression. Consider all the negative and frustrating experiences that can come with, for instance, password creation: failing to meet character requirements, failing to confirm the password by retyping it, inability to view the password as you type, CAPTCHA tedium, terms of service opt-ins, and more. Recently, I tried signing up for a service that required me to complete three separate CAPTCHA steps before I could finish creating my account. I can't tell you how many errors I made trying to find vehicles, stop signs, and traffic lights (**FIG 2.1**).

How many people do you believe will make it through such flows?

Whenever possible, defer prompts for creating an account until later in the onboarding experience, when the user is more likely to trust you and can understand the personal benefits of having an account. In Chapters 3 and 4, we'll look at how you can think about actions like creating an account in the context of the user onboarding journey.

Lack of inclusion

People from a range of backgrounds, situations, and abilities will come to your product, but might give up if you haven't done the work to include them. Inclusion, when it comes to onboarding newcomers, is about making sure that your product is able to meet people where they are; after all, onboarding is all about getting new users to stay, which may mean people from many new audiences! So we must, at the very least, have an experience that supports those with accessibility needs, who speak different languages, and who otherwise might not fit into a binary bucket.

- **Support assistive technology settings.** One of the biggest barriers you might be putting between your product and its new users is a lack of assistive support. For example, research firm Deque found that 70 percent of the websites they reviewed had "critical blockers" for visually impaired users, leading to abandonment and to revenue loss [7]. When new people arrive at your product, will they be met with a supportive or restrictive experience? Does your product support existing accessibility settings users may have set up for their device or browser, such as contrast settings or vibration settings? Does the first experience of your site or app make sense when read aloud by screen reader software?
- **Provide localization options.** No matter what markets we support, we should always expect new visitors from any combination of regional, cultural, or language backgrounds. We must ensure, at a minimum, they can understand our first-run experience. If possible, detect a user's region and

language settings on their device when they arrive and automatically switch your experience to reflect them; if you do not support their language or region, you can still use auto-detection to serve up a one-time message explaining this fact (and whether you ever plan to support it). If you can't auto-detect those settings upon their arrival, you can still find ways to make the experience welcoming to new users from different regions. For example, make it obvious where users can go to change their language or region settings. Check out the Resources section and take a look at *Cross-Cultural Design* by Senongo Akpem to start thinking about other ways to welcome users from various cultures and backgrounds.

- **Offer non-binary options.** If you ask new users to provide information or customize their experience, ensure the choices don't exclude entire audiences you would like to support. Asking people to put themselves in one category where multiple could apply (like "seller" vs "buyer") or restricting them to choices that don't respect their identities (like forcing a binary gender selection) can cause valued potential users to leave or have a negative first impression.

Hidden or unclear missions

Increasingly, people decide whether to use a product based on its organization's purpose and behaviors. According to a study by McKinsey, "Gen Z consumers are mostly well educated about brands and the realities behind them. When they are not, they know how to access information and develop a point of view quickly" [8].

Retailer Patagonia has built an avid following for its clothing products by investing in the ethical design and manufacturing of goods, and taking a public stance on issues ranging from sustainability to socially-progressive politics [9]. According to an article by Fast Company, the company's sales have increased fourfold in the decade during which they've been increasing their alignment with ethical production [10]. The company elevates its bold mission—"We're in business to save our home planet"—by dedicating a section of their website to their activ-

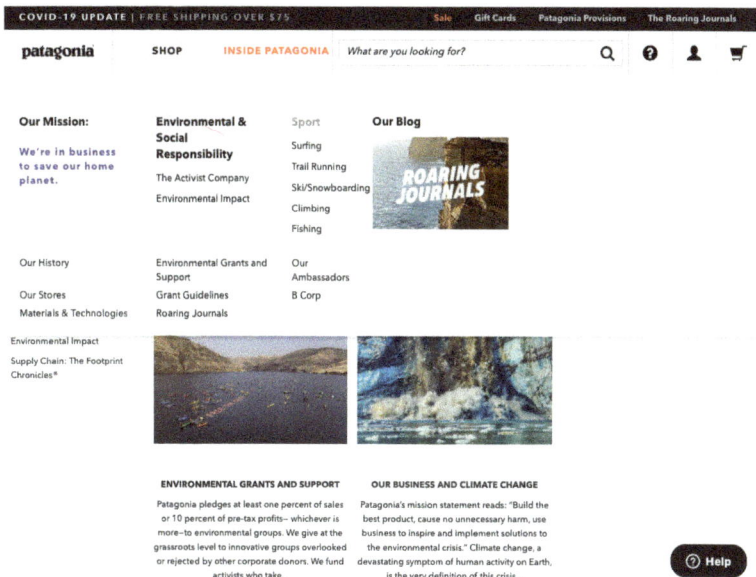

FIG 2.2: This screenshot from Patagonia shows how they've integrated their activist mission into their primary website navigation, which leads to a section about their mission statement and initiatives.

ist initiatives and including a link labeled "Activism" in their website's primary navigation, so it's front and center for new customers (**FIG 2.2**).

Of course, you may not be able to change your company's mission, but you can at least make it easier for your consumers to view the values your company embodies and make an informed decision for themselves. Within your product, provide clear access points to content like your organization's mission statement, operations, and leadership. If your company is active on social media, offering links to recent posts can provide transparency to new users about your current activities. If you make it difficult to access such content, people may feel you're intentionally trying to hide it and be put off from continuing with your product.

JUMPING (GRADUALLY) INTO ONBOARDING

Once you've convinced your team to invest in better user onboarding, given them a sense of the new user mindset, and started removing obvious roadblocks, you're ready to start designing for those promising new users we keep talking about. But we can't just throw everything at them all at once—we need to use guided interaction to break down their onboarding experience into manageable, meaningful parts. Our first stop is mapping the new user's journey.

3

MAPPING ONBOARDING JOURNEYS

WHEN I USED TO WORK on hardware setup flows, it was common for them to be viewed as prime pieces of real estate for all manner of tasks and content. I'd get requests to include legal, privacy, and system permissions, additional feature setup, add-on software installation, informational FYIs about things users would experience *after* setup, and promotional steps, like signing up for email updates. It was as if setup flows had a gravitational field where, the bigger the flow got, the more requests were pulled into its orbit.

Setup flows are not the only experiences that can suffer this fate. First-run experiences in general invite us to add "just one more thing" because of a misplaced hope we'll be able to transform a new user into a committed user in one go. But new users arrive in different situations and need to be able to move at their own pace. Onboarding is a journey of multiple actions that bridge the gap between a user's starting point and a sustainable, successful end state. First-run experiences often get overloaded when we don't see how the pieces can fit into such a journey.

Consider Airtasker, an Australian freelance job-posting product. There, it might be desirable for new folks to sign up and

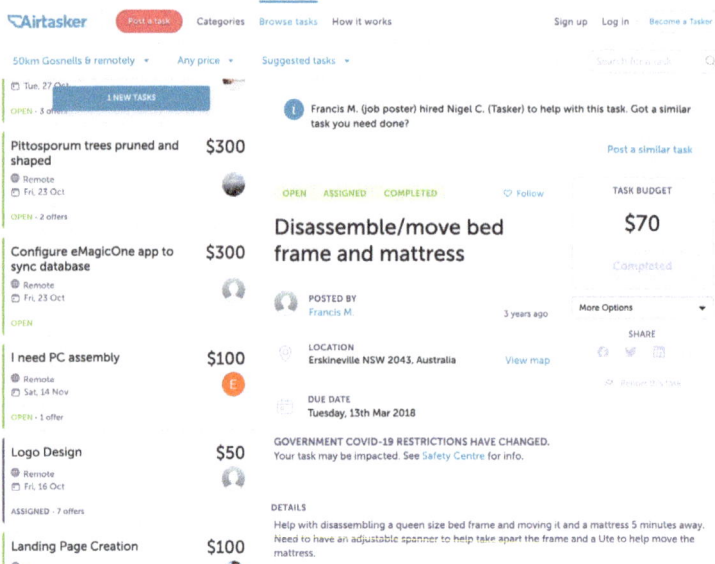

FIG 3.1: New visitors to the Airtasker website can view a selection of tasks before they've signed in, which serves as a jumping off point for multiple paths they can take afterward.

start posting a dozen jobs, which they call tasks, straight away. Instead, its website lets new users encounter various onboarding actions when the time is right for them. For example, newcomers can browse and "follow" tasks similar to the ones they are thinking of posting, familiarizing themselves with the platform and its process before becoming involved in the actions of posting a task and hiring someone (**FIG 3.1**). At any point, a newcomer can "skip ahead" to signing up or posting a job. But, by treating the onboarding journey as individual actions that might be encountered over time, Airtasker accommodates new users who might need more time to get up to speed (**FIG 3.2**).

This chapter will outline how to identify the actions new users might need to take during their onboarding journey in your product by mapping the user's path. This mapping involves:

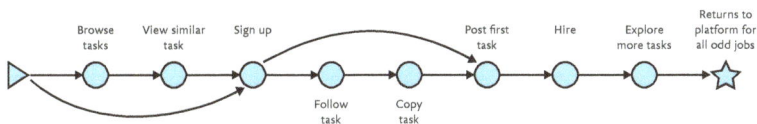

FIG 3.2: Using Airtasker as an example, we can see that a new user's onboarding journey can involve multiple actions, all of which can drive them to return to the service.

- defining the end state of onboarding,
- defining the entry situations of new users,
- working backward from end to entry,
- scoping actions appropriately, and
- prioritizing key actions for guidance.
  Let's look at each step of this mapping process in turn.

DEFINING THE END STATE

When do we consider a user successfully onboarded? What marks the end of their onboarding journey? Before we can figure out what guidance is needed to support users in their journey, we need to know how we're defining their destination.

I like the framing from designer Jonathan Korman, who said in a Twitter thread on first-time use:

If you begin with & focus on designing first-time use, it is hard to get to good solutions for long-term use. If you know the intermediate-use destination, you can strip stuff away to figure out what essentials to reveal for first-time use. [1]

His points are twofold: first, that understanding what intermediate use of your product looks like can lead to more success than focusing on first-time use. And, second, "intermediate" reminds us that our goal for every new user is *not* for them to become an expert—that type of thinking puts too much pressure on the onboarding journey and creates unrealistic expectations about our new users.

Onboarding's finish line *isn't* about making people an expert, much in the same way every new hire for a job isn't expected to become a CEO. The end state of onboarding is the point at which users are doing the activities that make them part of your core user base—what I call *core use*. Defining core use for your product will set the desired end-state for user onboarding.

Let's say we work on a product that helps people buy and sell pre-owned and restored goods online. As a company, our long-term goal might be to create a sustainable platform with a high quantity of transactions. Sellers are one of our primary users, and they may have long-term goals that range from making occasional supplemental income to building and running a full-time store.

For those users, we might define the core use of our product as:

Sells at least ten items per week while maintaining a high seller rating.

By regularly selling a reasonable quantity (ten) of high-quality items (represented by "high seller rating"), we've written a realistic and sustainable, yet aspirational, end-state for onboarding.

When defining core use for users of your product, make sure it's:

- **Aligned to long-term business goals:** A core user represents someone who is helping to sustain our business. Our definition of core use should therefore correlate to engagement, retention, or other product health goals, not a vanity metric like "has an account." "Sells at least ten items per week" gets at the kind of behavior that will sustain our business over time.
- **An achievable, desirable goal for the user:** Core use should be a state our users realistically can, and want to, be in. "Sells thirty-thousand items per week" would be great for us, but very few users could reasonably meet that state—and fewer still would want to be responsible for that much inventory! "Sells at least ten items per week" can include those rare,

prolific sellers, but is broad enough to apply to the majority of our user base.

- **Specific:** Your definition of core use shouldn't be generic, like "is retained" or "is satisfied." It needs to reflect whatever your business and user goals translate to—how successfully-onboarded users should interact with your product. "Sells ten items per week while maintaining a high seller rating" gives us a clear understanding of what success for onboarded users looks like: they'll be regularly selling items that makes buyers happy.
- **Framed around an individual user:** Your team may measure itself against a product health metric, such as "30 percent of sellers sell at least ten items per week." But it's too easy for the journeys of a new user to get lost in aggregate metrics. For the purposes of onboarding journeys, I frame core use around an individual. It's a small shift, but it can make a big difference in helping us visualize how a *single* person could take the journey to that state.
- **Independent of technology:** Avoid incorporating the technology people will use to meet their goals, such as, "Sells ten items *with the app* per week." This makes it hard for your onboarding experience to incorporate the range of technologies new users may try to use.

A product that serves many different audiences may need more than one definition of core use. For example, our imaginary selling platform must also support buyers; their core use statement might be something like, "Buys an item once a month."

Even if your product isn't as complex as an ecommerce platform, defining core use is an important step in onboarding design. For instance, onboarding for a printer doesn't just mean setting it up; it means getting a new printer owner to a state where they use the printer regularly, restock it with supplies from the printer company, and return to the same company for upgraded models.

DEFINING THE ENTRY SITUATIONS

We've specified our end state for onboarding with a core use definition and outlined the routines that support it. Now we need to define the entry situations that bring users to our product in the first place.

Entry situations are richer than just entry points (the channels that deliver users to a product, such as an emailed link, a social media post, an ad, a web search, etc.). A well-defined entry situation includes those things, but *also* includes the motivation and context the user brings with them. Their situation has a strong influence on what kinds of things they'd be interested in doing next.

Here are a few examples of potential entry situations for our fictional selling platform:

- While trying to get rid of a piece of clutter, a person found our website through an internet search. They're focused on using our product to sell that single item, so their onboarding journey needs to guide them to success with that one item, and *afterward* can inspire them to sell more.
- A person who specializes in restored items wants to set up a shop to sell them. They receive an invitation code for a free trial of our shop-hosting experience to see if we're a good fit. Because they already have the motivation to sell multiple items, it may take less time to get them to core use.
- A business or existing seller might want to move their existing inventory to our product. Their onboarding journey may need to focus on helping them import items from their existing digital or physical inventory.

An entry situation is often defined by user research, which can help you understand *why* users came to your product. And, if you have an existing product, your tracking analytics will tell you *how* users came to your product. If you've developed personas or user archetypes, you might look at those to extrapolate the kinds of scenarios that bring users in. All these investigations might reveal numerous entry situations because context and motivations can be nuanced. Seeing the range of situations that might bring new users to our products will help us understand how much variety we'll need to plan for in our onboarding journeys.

WORKING BACKWARD FROM END TO BEGINNING

Now let's fill in the actions that form the onboarding journey between a new user's entry situation and their core use. It might be tempting to start at the beginning and plot what path we assume a user should take from there. But, instead, we should start at the *end*. Working backward keeps us focused on the end state of onboarding and helps us break out a more complete set of actions than we might get if we started at the beginning.

Perhaps you or your team have created *journey maps* before—a birds-eye visualization of the different activities users do over time. If your team has a journey map, you may already have a decent view of your onboarding journey! An action-mapping exercise is very similar to journey mapping, albeit zoomed in a bit more on the onboarding path. I'll show you how I do this activity using a bullseye-style map.

Part 1: Set up your map and entry situations

On a large drawing space (such as a virtual whiteboard), draw three big concentric circles. In the centermost circle, write your core use definition. Outside of the largest circle, on opposing sides, write down two of your entry situations. Choose two that are common for your product, but different enough to reflect a range of situations (**FIG 3.3**).

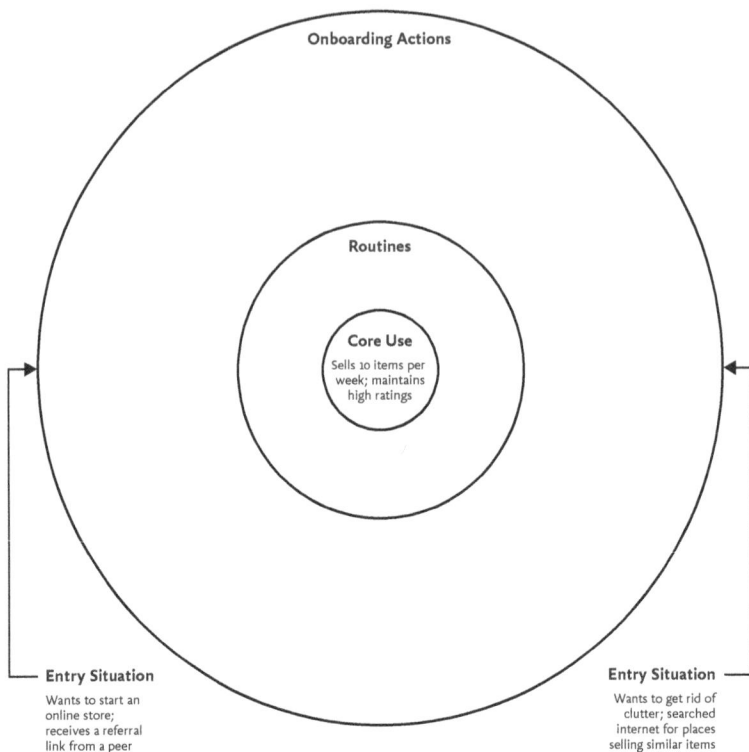

FIG 3.3: Put core use in the center of the smallest circle and entry situations on opposing sides of the largest circle.

Part 2: Add core use routines

Many definitions of core use will reflect a collection of recurring behaviors that core users do to stay successful. I call these recurring behaviors *core use routines*. Onboarding actions will build up to these behaviors, so we'll need to add that layer into our journey mapping exercise.

For example, core use sellers do more than just one thing to get from posting their first item for sale to selling ten items per week with high reviews. While posting multiple items each week is one routine they'd clearly have to maintain to reach a sustained number of sales, they may also be:

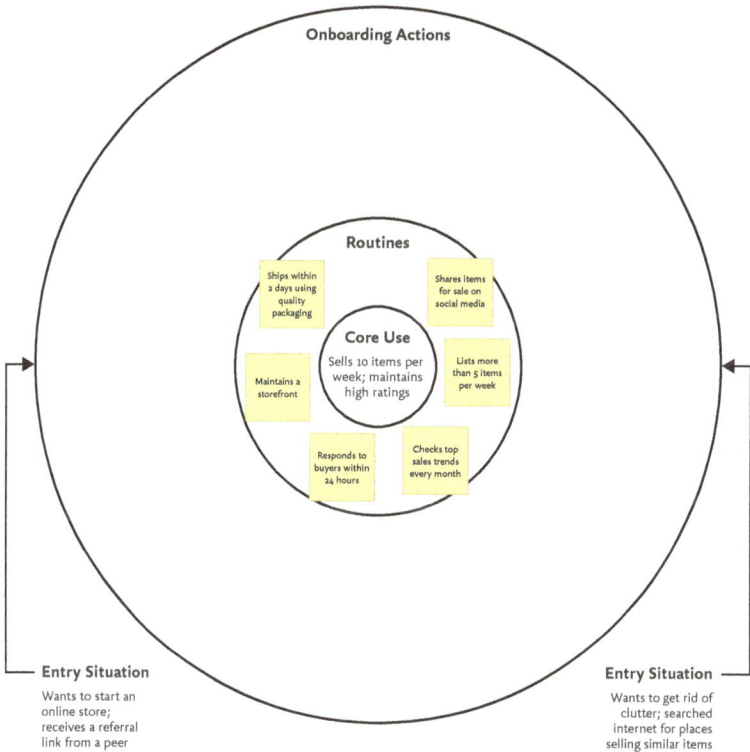

FIG 3.4: Identify three to six core use routines and put them in the middle circle, surrounding core use.

- responding to all messages from buyers within 24 hours, which results in better reviews and faster sales;
- maintaining a storefront, which organizes their inventory and attracts buyers; and
- checking out our monthly list of top-selling items, to keep on top of trends and get inspired about things to sell next.

Not every user may need to do every routine to be considered a core user, but these give us some specific routines to work backward from and keeps our team focused on the idea that onboarding actions are about building up to sustainable, recurring user activities, not one-off setups. So, for example, "creates an account" would *not* be a core use routine.

When you have a list of core use routines, choose three to six of the most common ones and add them to the middle circle, around the core use definition (**FIG 3.4**).

Part 3: Map the actions from core use routine to entry situation

To start mapping, choose one core use routine from the middle circle and:

1. Identify the action(s) users might have taken immediately prior to establishing the routine. Write this action in the largest circle, near the core use routine.
2. Now identify the action a user would have to take to reach the action you just wrote down and place it near the previous one.
3. Continue working backward in this manner to generate each action, working your way outward until you reach one of the entry situations (**FIG 3.5**).

Repeat these steps for different combinations of routines and entry situations until you end up with a constellation of actions in your biggest circle (**FIG 3.6**). Go ahead and repeat actions even if you've already written them down as part of a different combination, as the presence of the same action in multiple onboarding paths will be useful when it comes to prioritizing them!

Here's how that whole process might work for our hypothetical selling platform. We'll try mapping a path from the routine of "Responds to messages from buyers within 24 hours" and working out to the entry situation where someone has arrived from an internet search:

a) We know core sellers respond to messages more quickly when they are notified of new messages as soon as they arrive, so we write "Turn on mobile seller notifications."

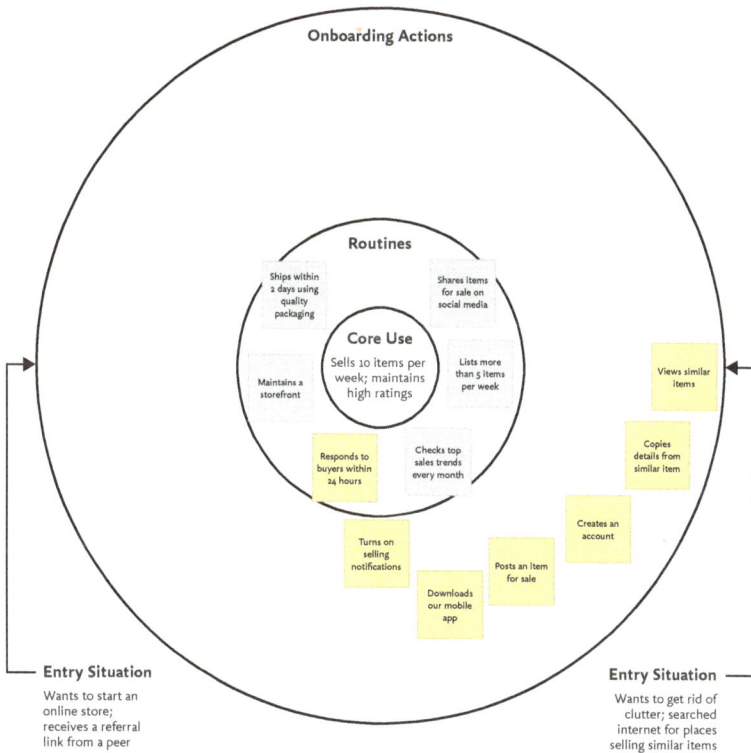

FIG 3.5: Work backward from one routine outward to an entry situation, then repeat for other routine and entry situation combinations.

b) To turn on mobile seller notifications, users need our mobile app. Write "Download the app."

c) But we don't just start peppering incoming new users with prompts to get our app! We need to think about the kind of previous experience that would have justified a user turning on notifications and, thus, getting the app to do so. In looking at the analytics of our existing core sellers, we might find most of them downloaded the app after posting an item for sale. Write down "Post first item for sale."

d) Users can't post something for sale without having a seller account, so we jot down "Creates a seller account."

Onboarding Actions

Routines

Core Use
Sells 10 items per week; maintains high ratings

Downloads our mobile app

Sets up bill autopay

Saves shipping preferences

Posts first item for sale

Connects a social media account

Enables automatic sharing to social media

Connects a billing payment method

Ships items at the same time every week

Turns on selling notifications

Posts first item for sale

Adds seller profile photos

Ships within 2 days using quality packaging

Shares items for sale on social media

Turns on automatic relisting of unsold items

Saves item posted for sale as a template

Posts first item for sale

Compares our fees to other services

Imports existing inventory

Downloads app

Lists more than 5 items per week

Creates item templates

Views similar items

Signs up for a free trial of our shop-building experience

Sets up basic shop information

Maintains a storefront

Pays first shop bill

Creates an account

Customizes shop theme

Responds to buyers within 24 hours

Checks top sales trends every month

Browses top selling items page

Copies details from similar item

Posts first item for sale

Selects a preset shop template

Creates templates

Subscribes for top selling trends updates

Creates an account

Sets up basic seller profile

Turns on selling notifications

Sells first item

Downloads app

Post san item for sale

Turns on shop notifications

Ships first item

Sells first item

Saves shipping preferences for later

Entry Situation
Wants to start an online store; receives a referral link from a peer

Entry Situation
Wants to get rid of clutter; searched internet for places selling similar items

FIG 3.6: Fill in the larger circle with a constellation of key actions you can then prioritize and scope.

e) Now, looking at our user research or analytics might reveal another onboarding action that came before this point—the user jumpstarting their first post by looking at similar items on our site and choosing to copy some of the information over to one of their own. So, we add "Start a new post with details copied from a similar item."

f) This means, of course, that people were "viewing similar items to one they want to sell." And that's what brings us to back to our entry situation, where someone has arrived on our website after searching the internet for similar items.

You could probably think of even more actions that could go between any one of these. That's fine! This exercise is all about revealing that a person's onboarding journey can involve more than one step; those who might have been tempted to pelt newly-arrived users with "enable notifications" or "download our app!" prompts can see how those would work better in the context of other actions being completed first.

An added benefit of this exercise is that it can help your team visualize the different paths people need to take as they develop into core users of our product, based on different routines and entry situations. The journey from this searches-for-similar-items person might be much longer if they need to build up the routine of "checks our top sales trends every week," since that might require them to experience other successes first. Whereas for those who came to our product with an intent to create a shop, they may take a more direct journey to routines like checking our top sales trends every week or maintaining a storefront.

SCOPING ACTIONS

Now that we have a large collection of potential user actions, we need to examine the scope of what each action will achieve in more detail. An action like "Subscribes to newsletter," for example, only needs the user to complete one task (entering an email address). But an action like "Posts an item for sale" would involve several related tasks, such as creating an account, adding item details, taking photos of the item, and setting up payment and shipping details.

Both of these actions are appropriately scoped given what they need to achieve, even if one is "bigger" than the other. While there's no one single way to scope an action in our onboarding experience, I like how GOV.UK frames scoping:

Scoping your transaction means deciding what the transaction does and doesn't do, and which problem it solves for users.

If you scope your transaction too broadly or try to make it do too many things, it won't be obvious what problem it's

*solving. And users won't be able to get straight to the task they
need to complete.*

*If the scope is too narrow, the transaction won't fully solve
the user's problem, meaning they don't get the outcome
they need.* [2]

As you look at the actions from your mapping exercise, make
sure they represent a self-contained scope that will move users
forward in their experience. Properly scoped actions:

- **Provide a noticeable benefit to the user upon completion.**
  If an action contains tasks that aren't noticeably applied to
  the product after the action is done, or if it includes many
  optional subtasks, it may be time to separate those tasks
  or omit them entirely. For example, if you ask the user to
  indicate what industry they work in, but their answer has
  no discernable effect on the content or features, then that
  request isn't in scope for an onboarding action. If the user
  won't see the benefit immediately, it likely doesn't belong.
- **Include the work needed to get the job done.** If you've
  brainstormed two separate actions that must always follow each other because they are interdependent, consider
  merging them into a single action. This way, you'll design
  the flow through them seamlessly, whereas, if you design
  each action independently, users might experience a clunky,
  inconsistent transition between them.
- **Reflect the user's definition of the action.** Sometimes our
  organization's definition of the work that needs to be done
  in an action is out of sync with what a user expects. For
  example, our imaginary selling platform team may interpret
  "create an account" as "creating an account, completing a
  seller profile, and filling in demographic information" but
  the user may simply take it to mean, "this will just be about
  creating a login so I can return to my items for sale later."

PRIORITIZING ONBOARDING ACTIONS

When you work backward between different start and end-points, you'll inevitably think up many potential actions your onboarding journey might include. And that's great, because it's much better than being too focused on one single flow or action.

That said, it's not desirable (or feasible!) for an onboarding journey to emphasize every possible action with equal weight. What you choose to emphasize is, in itself, a form of guidance about what's important, so let's prioritize the actions that need the most support.

After you've identified possible actions, using the following criteria to review them can help you focus on the most important actions through which people need to be guided:

- **Which actions reduce abandonment or failure?** Are there certain actions you've identified that, if not done, will lead to abandonment or failure to reach core use? For example, we want to avoid a new user starting to list an item, and then abandoning it before it gets posted for sale. Digging into research might show us that many abandoned posts were started by new users who tried to create one from scratch. This would indicate the action of "Copy details from a similar item" is a high priority for us to emphasize to new users.
- If you find that people who don't complete one or more key actions within a window of time are less successful overall, then this is a signal to prioritize them. For example, Twitter found retention was higher when users followed thirty people, so they emphasized the action of following others early on in a new user's experience [3]. Be cautious, however, about strictly timeboxing when an action needs to be encountered. Some teams hyper-focus on finding the perfect formula for getting new users to do [one big thing] in their first [n] days, but that's a recipe for failure when people don't behave on a prescribed schedule. Just focus on which actions need to come earlier rather than later.

- **Which actions are required to do other key actions?** Some actions are going to be obvious or necessary based on how your product is set up. For example, in our hypothetical selling service, maybe a user doesn't need to create an account to browse products, but they will eventually need one in order to sell an item. Therefore, we'll need to include this in our list of prioritized actions, even if it doesn't have to happen first.
- **Which actions are useful for many different entry situations?** If your mapping activity showed that the same action came up multiple times in different permutations of core use routines and entry situations, that's a signal it should be prioritized.
- **Which actions can you realistically support?** In the course of the mapping activity, you might outline actions not yet offered by your product, or are outside of your immediate control. These are great ideas to capture, since they might contribute to future plans for your product; mapping your onboarding journey can often reveal gaps in what your product offers today. But if you can't implement these ideas, set them aside, and focus on those actions you *do* have control over.

DESTINATION-DRIVEN ONBOARDING

A good onboarding journey is not a single flow that happens all during first run. It's made up of multiple actions that bridge the gap between a user's entry state and an end state of core use. Mapping these actions by working backward from the end ensures we're thinking about guiding new users to a clear destination, even if their paths to get there are different. Finally, scoping and prioritizing our actions means we know which key moments we should invest our onboarding efforts in.

Now that we've identified our important onboarding actions, we can provide new users with guidance anchored to meaningful interaction—and that moves users from one action to another. The next chapter will help us break down how to do just that.

4 GUIDANCE IN ACTION

AFTER MAPPING OUT YOUR ONBOARDING JOURNEY, you'll find yourself with a prioritized list of the multiple, important actions that plug into a new user's path to core use. While your team will have a birds-eye view of the onboarding journey, your new users will be experiencing your product on an action-by-action basis. The guidance you offer will need to help new users complete the action at hand while also connecting the dots into the larger journey.

We can break onboarding actions down into three parts, making it easier to see where we can anchor such guidance (**FIG 4.1**):

- The *prompt* to take action at the beginning;
- the *work* involved in the middle of the action;
- and the *follow-up* at the end of the action.

This structure helps us think about designing actions like modules that have multiple entry and exit points depending on where they are dropped in.

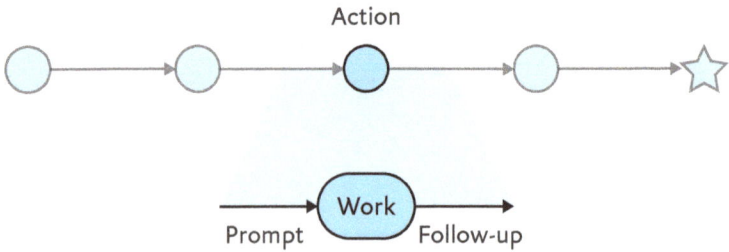

FIG 4.1: Any single onboarding action can be broken down into a prompt (or prompts) that lead into it, the work of the action itself in the middle, and a follow-up moment that leads a user onward to the next action(s) in their journey.

Let's look at an example. I used to contribute to a prior version of the eBay Motors iOS app, which was tailored to automotive aficionados who bought parts for their vehicles. One of the actions that improved the experience of new users was that of saving the make and model of a vehicle they owned to the app, as it helped them quickly find compatible parts to purchase. The action was structured in three parts, which guided new users to complete it right away:

- Upon opening, the app prompted users to identify their vehicle while explicitly stating the benefit of finding matching parts and accessories (the prompt);
- then, users would specify the attributes of their vehicle, like year, make, and model (the work); and finally
- users were redirected to the app's home screen, which showed an entry point to finding parts matching their vehicle, as well as a confirmation message that indicated where they could access their saved vehicle in the future (the follow-up) **(FIG 4.2)**.

It might seem like using this three-segment approach could add *unnecessary* structure to "straightforward" onboarding actions, such as those that prompt people to subscribe to an

FIG 4.2: These screenshots from an older version of the eBay Motors iOS app show the onboarding action of saving a new user's vehicle broken into a flow of three composite parts: the prompt, a full screen upon first app launch which encourages the user to save a vehicle they own (left); the work, which involves inputting information (middle); and the follow-up, which confirms success and next steps in the form of an entry point to find parts for that vehicle (right).

email. But this isn't about adding guidance for guidance's sake; instead, segmentation helps us consider the different contexts in which a new user might encounter a task, so we can determine how much structure is truly needed for the task to feel accomplishable.

Consider how ProPublica guides people through the straightforward action of subscribing to its Big Story emails (**FIG 4.3**). There are only subtle differences between the initial prompt, the work, and follow-up because they're all handled by different states of an email subscription box embedded in an article: the prompt is the initial state of the email field, the work is the state as the user is typing their email address; and the follow-up is the confirmation message after the user taps "Sign Up."

To figure out what kind of guidance you might need throughout your important onboarding actions, let's break down each of the three segments.

ne told me. I don't know, to be clear, it occurring situation. I have no idea."

Get Our Top Investigations
Subscribe to the Big Story newsletter.

[Enter your email]

[Sign Up]

This site is protected by reCAPTCHA and the Google Privacy Policy and Terms of Service apply.

Ther
panc
used
liber
polit
have
said.

He h
That
panc

catastrophe. Our country wasn't prepar
our top leaders has been disjointed. We

ProPublica

ne told me. I don't know, to be clear, it occurring situation. I have no idea."

Get Our Top Investigations
Subscribe to the Big Story newsletter.

[ ]

[Sign Up]

This site is protected by reCAPTCHA and the Google Privacy Policy and Terms of Service apply.

Ther
panc
used
liber
polit
have
said.

He h
That
panc

catastrophe. Our country wasn't prepar
our top leaders has been disjointed. We'

ProPublica

ne told me. I don't know, to be clear, it occurring situation. I have no idea."

Get Our Top Investigations
Subscribe to the Big Story newsletter.

[ ]

[You're signed up!]

This site is protected by reCAPTCHA and the Google Privacy Policy and Terms of Service apply.

Ther
panc
used
liber
polit
have
said.

He h
That
panc

catastrophe. Our country wasn't prepar
our top leaders has been disjointed. We'

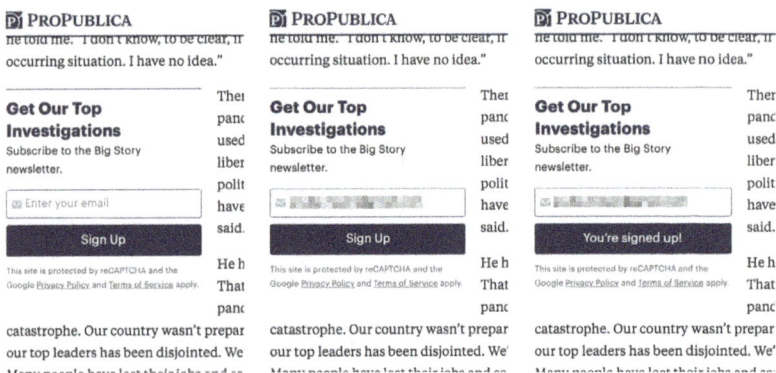

FIG 4.3: The prompt (left), work (middle), and follow-up states (right) of ProPublica's subscription action are each detectable, but seamlessly interconnected in the flow so they don't disrupt the user's experience.

PROMPTS: MAKING THE CASE

A prompt is any mechanism the user acts on to initiate an action. It can come in a variety of forms, from something as simple as a text link in product navigation to something as prominent as a full-screen request. To design a prompt that provides the right amount of guidance so new users can decide to take action, we need to:

- Pick the right context
- Align to user benefit
- Set expectations
- Consider your "free samples"
  Let's look at each of these items in more detail.

Pick the right context

When is the most meaningful time and place for a new user to start an onboarding action, and finish it successfully? The more confidence we have that an action is relevant to and achievable by a user at a given time, the more we can encourage them to act. The less confident we are that an action is relevant to and achievable by a user in that situation, the less we should encourage them to act. The answer to this question will help you decide how a prompt should look and act.

The prompt in the eBay Motors example has prominent treatment: a full screen displayed on first run suggested a high degree of confidence that new users were shopping for parts for their own vehicle. On the other hand, the ProPublica example uses a fairly lightweight prompt. It isn't pushing the user to take action, since the user may or may not have any interest in reading more content from the same source. You might find there are different contexts in which it makes sense to prompt users to take action, and in these cases, you can plan on having different prompt treatments for the same action.

Contextual cues can come from many sources, such as time, date, and even prior work completed. For example, I once asked Alexa, a voice service by Amazon, for the day's weather in the morning, and Alexa followed the weather report with this prompt: "By the way, I can help you get the day started on the right note. Would you like me to play music?" Playing music is a key feature of the device and it stands to reason it would make sense for setting up music to be a prioritized onboarding action. Prompting a person to do that after another start-the-day action means the request is more relevant and reasonable than, say, suggesting users to set up music after setting a timer.

When we adjust the strength of a prompt to match a user's context, we also implicitly make the case for them to take action. Just be aware that some contexts require explicit user consent (such as location permission) that may not be worth requesting if only for the purpose of showing tailored prompts later in the experience.

Align to user benefit

Align any copy, imagery, or content around the benefit of taking action to make a compelling case. You don't need to write a book about the many benefits of an action or your product's features to achieve this. This is where some clear and user-focused content can come in.

For example, in the eBay Motors app, the action the prompt was asking users to take—"Tell us what you drive"—was accompanied by a line of benefit: "We'll help you find parts and accessories for your vehicle." and showed images of different vehicle types to indicate that a range of vehicles was supported. While there might be other benefits associated with this action, this prompt focuses on the one that will be immediately noticeable once the user completes the action. Having contextual cues about a user's situation allows you to tailor the user benefit even more. For example, once a user's vehicle is saved, the benefits for other onboarding actions can be written in a way that's personalized to that vehicle.

When sharing the benefits of an action, remember these are new users who don't know all the names of your features. So, don't frame your benefits around concepts users haven't interacted with yet. eBay Motors didn't introduce the concept of "The Garage" until after a new user saved their vehicle or arrived at the app's home screen.

Set expectations

Convincing users to take action also involves setting clear expectations at the start, either to reassure them that the work ahead won't be long or arduous, or to prepare them for when the work of the action is more involved.

On many prompts, this kind of expectation-setting can be achieved with clear copy and action labels. A button labeled "Turn on notifications," for example, likely suggests a speedy result, while "Set up notification preferences" implies something that will take more time and decision-making. As we noted in the previous chapter on scoping actions, users may expect certain actions to include a certain set of work. Make sure your copy reflects that understanding.

For actions that require substantial time, effort, or information, it's helpful to give a preview of the work that might be involved, or mention any prerequisites, so users don't start down a path only to be surprised by extra work. For example, when asking users to install software, tell them to charge their device before getting started.

Consider your "free samples"

When we consider how we need to set the stage for prompting an onboarding action, it's clear that, the more context a user has, the easier it will be to prompt them to take an action, to align the action to their benefit, and to set good expectations. This is especially important if your product requires users to sign up.

Instead of forcing people to make a commitment to your product too early, give them a *free sample*: a commitment-free taste of your product's value proposition that is usable before an account is necessary.

Being able to use a portion of your product commitment-free gives your new users the context they need to make informed decisions about acting on a prompt, while also providing a positive first impression. Perhaps one of the best examples of the power of free samples is from Jared Spool's case study "The $300 Million Button," which showed how enabling guest checkout—and asking people to sign up after—led to an increase of $300 million in sales [1].

Graphic design platform Canva lets new, unregistered users of its website compose materials, like flyers or cards, and even download them, without an account. Users are not prompted to create an account until they want to print or save something to edit later (**FIG 4.4**).

If your product involves subscriptions as part of its commitment, you can extend the concept of a free sample with a free trial experience. Magic Seaweed is a service that provides ocean condition forecasts for surfers and other folks. New users can see the next seven-day forecast without an account, but the sixteen-day forecast is locked behind a pro subscription wall (which offers access to a free trial of the pro version) (**FIG 4.5**).

With this approach, ensure the user is not inadvertently hitting a prompt at every turn; that will get old, fast. Be selective about how many parts of your product will prompt for a commitment. And, while this may be tempting, don't let a user create a lot of content during a free sample experience only to tell them they'll lose it all if they don't make a commitment to an account. There goes your positive first impression!

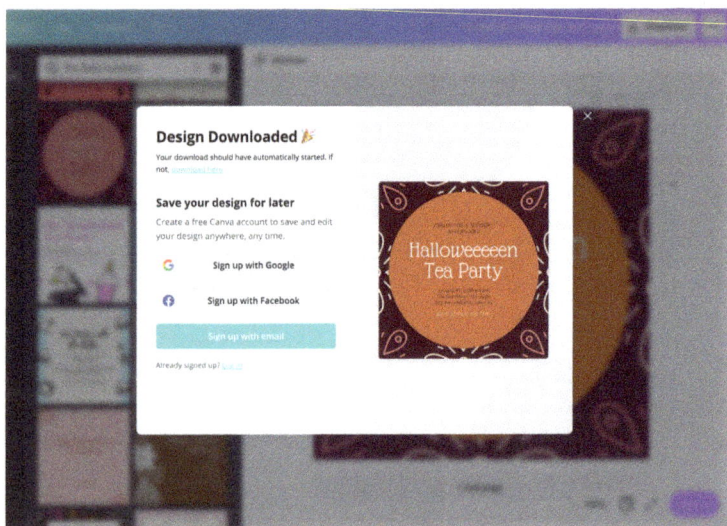

FIG 4.4: The Canva website lets new users create and download their own designs without signing up for an account. The signup prompt is then framed around saving the designs to edit later.

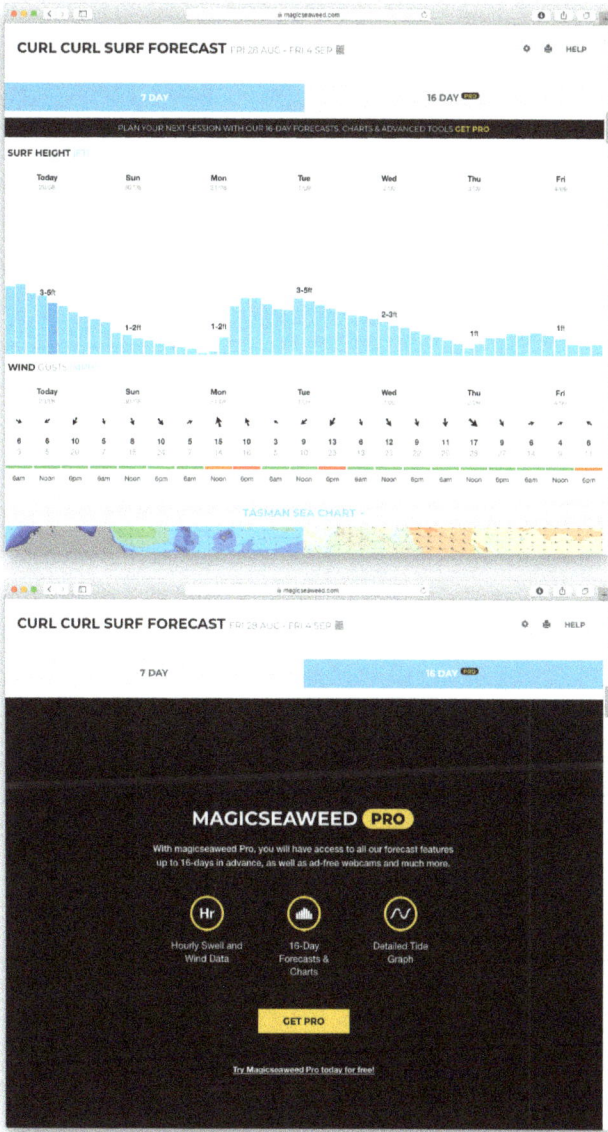

FIG 4.5: Even without an account or subscription, users can access a seven-day forecast and surf data. Once they try to access the sixteen-day forecast, they're prompted to sign up for the pro version.

It's worth noting that trials for paid products also bear the risk that one person will create many fake accounts to effectively get months of free, full access. In this case, it's up to your team to decide if this would represent a material loss, and come up with an alternative free sample. For example, a video streaming service concerned with people abusing its free trials can consider letting users browse their complete list of titles before they're asked to sign up.

GUIDING THROUGH THE WORK

After a prompt is initiated, we end up in the work of the action. Guiding people through this means we have to:

- create continuity,
- provide support in context,
- offer alternatives, and
- make errors actionable and informative.

Create continuity

When a user acts on a prompt, the state they encounter next should reflect the same benefits, goals, and expectations that got them to take action in the first place. Otherwise, the user may feel misled or confused.

Using similar language and imagery across the prompt and the work of an action can provide continuity. For example, Australian real estate company Domain prompts new users who search for homes to turn on property alerts to receive updates about their search. The work of turning on property alerts requires choosing the alert frequency and signing up for an account. Domain makes continuous references to the benefits of property alerts across all screens in this signup flow, expanding on the benefits and details as the user progresses (**FIG 4.6**). Meanwhile, if a user came to the signup flow from a prompt to save a property, the messaging in this flow changes to reflect their goal of saving a property. This continuity of messaging across the work of the action gives new users confidence that,

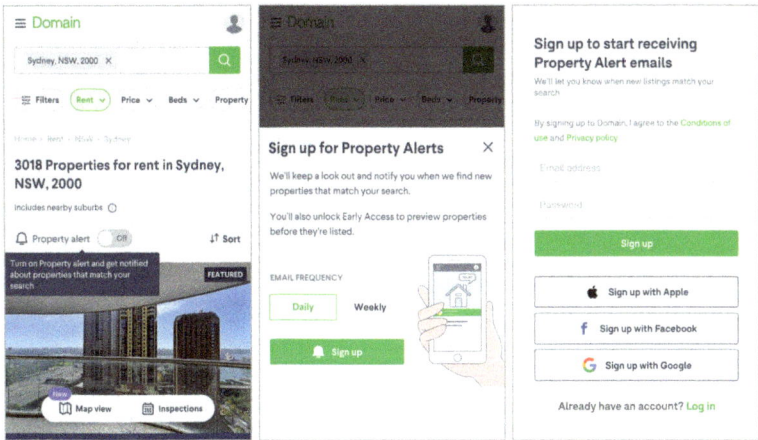

FIG 4.6: When new users on Domain are prompted to enable alerts and create an account, the prompt language is reiterated across the flow.

by the end of the work, the task they initially set out to accomplish will be finished.

Provide support in context

To guide a user through the action, make sure any supporting information that will help them complete the work is available at the point of doing the work itself. For example, verifying an ID is one of the onboarding actions for new users of international money transfer app TransferWise. Instructions and a visual guide are presented in the context of the camera screen itself, not separated on a screen that appears beforehand (**FIG 4.7**).

If you need to provide further details that don't all fit (or would be overwhelming) on a single screen, offer a way for users to see that extra information without leaving their current flow. That's what freelance job website Airtasker does: it offers a "Want help?" button when someone is pricing a job, which expands a list of suggested price ranges on the current screen (**FIG 4.8**).

FIG 4.7: The mobile app for TransferWise provides tips in the context of the camera screen to help users line up and take an accurate photograph of their ID.

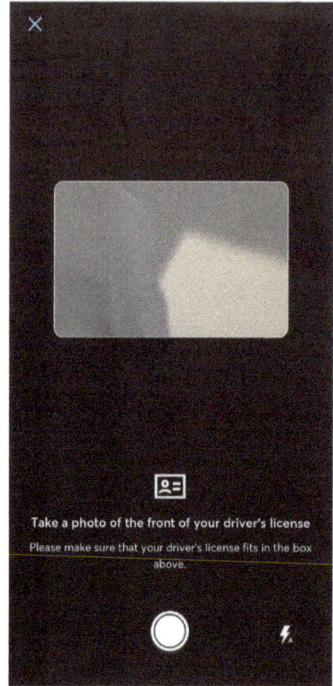

Take a photo of the front of your driver's license

Please make sure that your driver's license fits in the box above.

Some onboarding actions may be made up of multiple pieces of work, called *subtasks*, that come together to achieve the action's goal. For example, the "post first job" action on Airtasker includes the subtasks of specifying the type of job, pricing the job, and describing the job. We can provide contextual, focused support for subtasks by organizing them into groups.

Sometimes, we can disclose all the subtasks of an action together on the same screen by visually organizing them into groups. This is better when actions can all be done simultaneously, when the choices of one group don't change the choices of another group, and when the number of subtasks won't overwhelm a new user or lead to awkward scrolling on smaller screens. The eBay Motors app organized the subtasks of selecting vehicle type, year, make and model together on the same screen, for example.

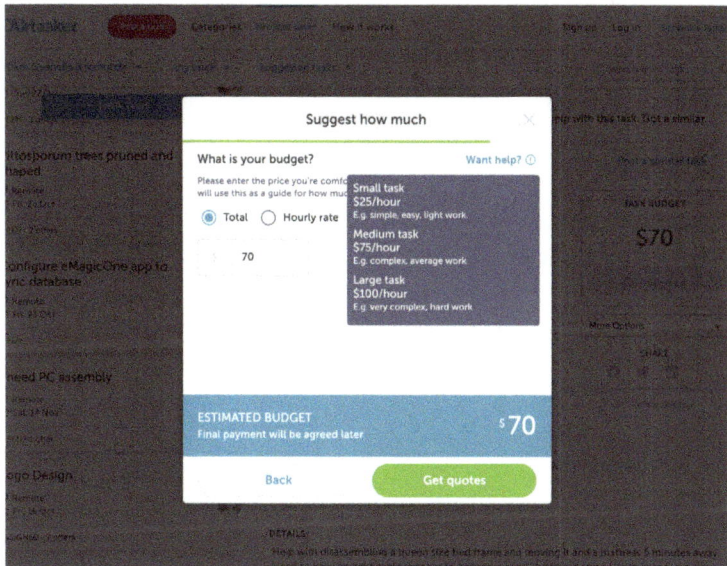

FIG 4.8: This flow for posting a new job on the Airtasker website provides supplemental guidance for pricing a job under a "Want help?" button.

But another approach is to *sequence* the guidance of our onboarding action by organizing its subtasks into a series of steps that are revealed in a linear progression. This is good when you have subtasks that depend on others being completed first, when you have a logical progression of steps, or when each subtask would benefit from focused support.

For example, the workout app Seven uses a sequenced approach to its onboarding action of setting up a fitness plan. The flow guides users from a broad choice at the start (choosing their overall fitness goals) to narrower choices at the end (opting in to be reminded to work out at a specific time every day) (**FIG 4.9**). Sequenced guidance can take other forms as well, such as in conversational interfaces like chats, or a single screen that progressively reveals new sections as subtasks if previous sections are completed.

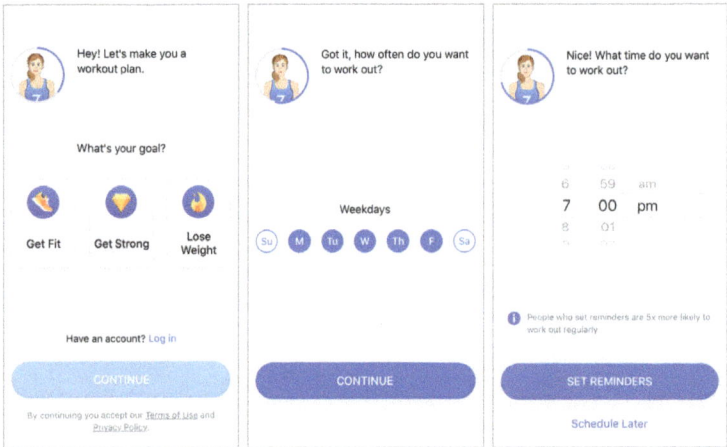

FIG 4.9: Seven's onboarding action is structured as a sequenced flow that guides new users through setting up a fitness goal, setting up their weekly workout schedule, and scheduling workout reminders. A circular progress meter (upper left of each screenshot) signposts the progress through the flow.

The more subtasks your action includes, the more time and effort it can require from the user. In addition to making sure your action already represents well-scoped work (if it doesn't, pop back into the previous chapter's section on scoping actions before proceeding!), keep the following in mind:

- **Differentiate required subtasks from optional subtasks, and order them so the required ones are disclosed first,** no matter how you choose to disclose the subtasks of your onboarding action. Even in a well-scoped action, it's possible there might be a few subtasks that are optional or can be done later. Put required items before the optional ones so that a user can see the most important things they need to do straight away.

- **Show progress with clear, determinate signposting when using a sequenced approach.** Sometimes we get hung up on judging a flow by the number of screens, clicks, or taps involved, thinking that more is worse, when the issue might be due to a lack of signposting.

  New users need to see a light at the end of the tunnel to stay motivated. Use determinate progress indicators that show how much work has been completed and how much work remains. You can use pagination when you always know the exact number of steps that will be involved, and you can use a visual indicator like a progress bar either when you know an exact number of steps, or when you might have a rough approximation (for example, if one step may not appear based on a choice made in a previous step).

- **Avoid subtasks that must be completed out of the context of the flow.** Don't add subtasks to an action that requires users to leave the current flow and complete a step elsewhere in order to continue. This is far too common in apps that, for example, ask users to verify their email address by opening their email program, finding an email from the company, and clicking a link in it. But these detours can lead users to abandon the action and never return to complete it.

  If you must include something like email verification, consider the approach that form-creation tool Typeform has taken, where users can verify their email *after* they finish the action of creating an account. Users are given clear instructions on how to retrieve the message along with options to switch the account's email address or get more help (**FIG 4.10**). Other products that require email verification might even let new users continue using the product with limited functionality until they verify their address.

For a deeper dive on different considerations for organizing subtasks in a sequenced manner, check out the Resources section.

FIG 4.10: The Typeform signup process requires email verification, but it specifies details and provides a link to a support article if the user needs help.

Offer alternatives

We can increase the odds that users will successfully complete an onboarding action by offering alternative routes to success. Seeing that alternatives are available gives people added reassurance that they'll be able to complete an action at a time that's right for them. We can approach alternatives in a few ways:

- **Give users a different way to complete an action than the primary method suggested.** For example, an account signup flow might emphasize social login, but also show options to create an account using a phone number or email address for those without, or who choose not to use, a social account.
- **Give users the option to skip part of the work.** For example, in the Seven workout app, users had the option to schedule their workout reminders later instead of during the app's setup flow. Letting them defer this optional step prevents them from getting into a bad state by hastily denying notifications permission.

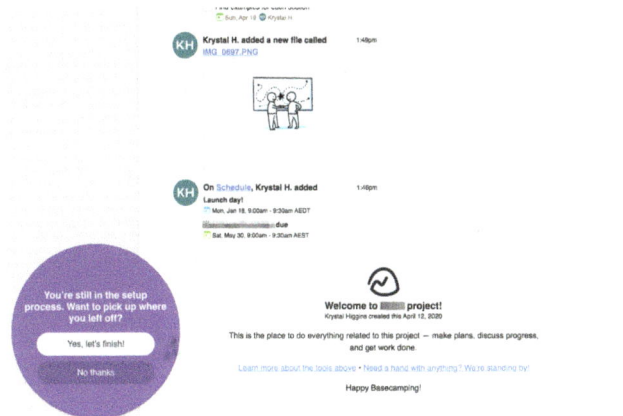

FIG 4.11: Basecamp Personal shows new users a reminder if they've left project setup prematurely, reassuring them that they can pick up where they left off.

- **Let users save progress and return later.** Letting people save and return later is especially important for onboarding actions that ask a new user to invest a lot of time and effort. Otherwise, you might have a hard time convincing them to make the investment in the first place! Everything from system errors to human distraction are all common scenarios that can force users to leave and return later. One option is to automatically save the work on the user's behalf, and inform them that their progress has been saved. In other cases, you can provide a manual save option for those who choose to leave an action prematurely. For example, in Basecamp Personal, a virtual project management tool, users who leave the action of project setup prematurely may jump right back to where they left off (**FIG 4.11**). For new users who do not have an account or are otherwise offline, their progress can be saved to local device storage [2]; and there are other ways to save drafts of content, like storing it at a unique URL and letting users send that link to their email.

Make errors actionable and informative

Providing continuity, contextual guidance, and alternatives for completing onboarding actions all help reduce the chance that users will encounter an error, while also guiding them in ways that are flexible and supportive. But no matter how well we design our onboarding actions, a new user will, in all likelihood, eventually run into an error.

We need to design errors in ways that are informative and actionable. Errors are valuable opportunities to demonstrate what a product can do for a new user, especially since negative experiences tend to be more memorable than unremarkable ones [3].

When new users encounter errors, we need to:

- be clear about why the error occurred;
- give actionable options for resolving it, where possible; and
- connect people to additional resources, when available.

For example, the TransferWise app provides an informative error if the user takes a photo of an unrecognizable ID. The error message provides specific details on why the image didn't pass the verification requirements, with an action to take another picture (**FIG 4.12**). This gives the user tailored information they can use to try for a different result right away, and avoids forcing all users, including those who might never experience an issue, to read a list of all error-preventing instructions up front.

Now, once the work of an onboarding action is successfully completed, we move into the follow-up state.

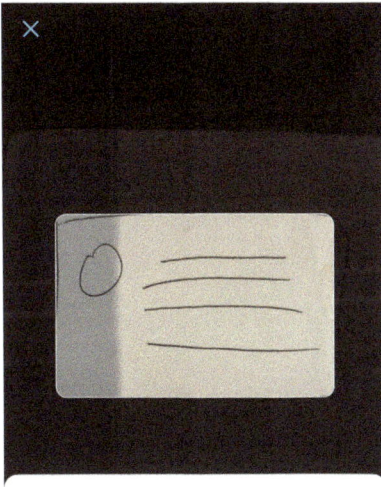

FIG 4.12: TransferWise's informative error message provides detailed feedback and an option to redo the action that led to the error.

The error screen shows:

Sorry, there was a problem

☹ We couldn't read everything that was printed on your ID. Please make sure nothing is covering it.

☹ We couldn't see an ID in the photo. Please take a photo of your driver's licence, national ID card, or passport photo page.

☹ We couldn't see the front of your ID.

Take a new picture

FOLLOW-UP: CONNECTING THE DOTS

The *follow-up* is what closes out an action. The follow-up state requires us to:

- Acknowledge success
- Provide meaningful next steps

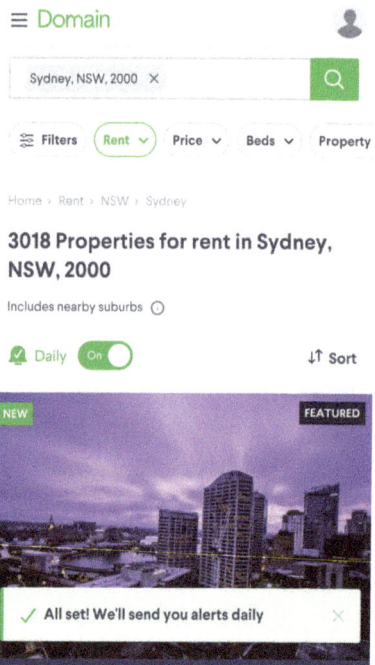

FIG 4.13: Domain uses both a temporary confirmation message and a persistent alert status to reiterate the user's selected notification frequency.

Acknowledge success

Provide feedback indicating a new user has completed an onboarding action successfully. This will give them a sense of progress, while also underlining the purpose of the completed action, letting us end an onboarding action on a feelgood moment.

Success can be acknowledged with any kind of state change: small confirmation animations, redirections to new or updated product screens, and full screen celebratory messages are just a few approaches. The follow-up state that appears after a user has enabled property alerts on Australian real estate website Domain acknowledges success with a brief confirmation banner at the bottom of the screen, as well as by showing the alerts toggle in the "on" state (**FIG 4.13**). This confirmation closes the loop started by the prompt the user acted on initially.

The significance of the work done in the action defines how strongly we should acknowledge success. A straightforward action that doesn't involve heavy investment may need nothing more than some lightweight feedback or a redirection to a new screen; over-emphasizing the success would be disruptive. Meanwhile, an action that is critical or involves heavy investment may deserve a more prominent celebration; underemphasizing the success can leave users wondering if the work they did was actually impactful.

Provide meaningful next steps

Another way we provide feedback after a completed onboarding action is by illustrating any next steps that will connect a new user from the action they just completed to other actions in their broader onboarding journey. Next steps are essential to creating an onboarding experience that flows.

Next steps should be meaningful to the user and should reflect the actions they have already accomplished. Workout app Seven has two onboarding actions, and each shows next steps in different ways that fit the context of the action completed. After setting up a workout plan, a new user is redirected to the app's home screen, which implies the next step is to begin their first workout. After completing the onboarding action of their first workout, however, next steps are explicitly listed on a dedicated screen and reflect settings the user hasn't yet enabled (**FIG 4.14**).

When designing next steps, it's easy to get a little overzealous. We certainly want to re-engage new users, but not at risk of overwhelming them! It's important to make sure your next steps are relevant and focused on what benefits the user.

To keep next steps relevant, avoid the following pitfalls:

- **Don't use catchall checklists.** A checklist often invites a team to write down their wish list of features they'd like a new user to do, but may not represent the real next steps most new users would need to take during an onboarding journey. If a checklist includes activities some users don't need to do, it can render the rest of the list meaningless by

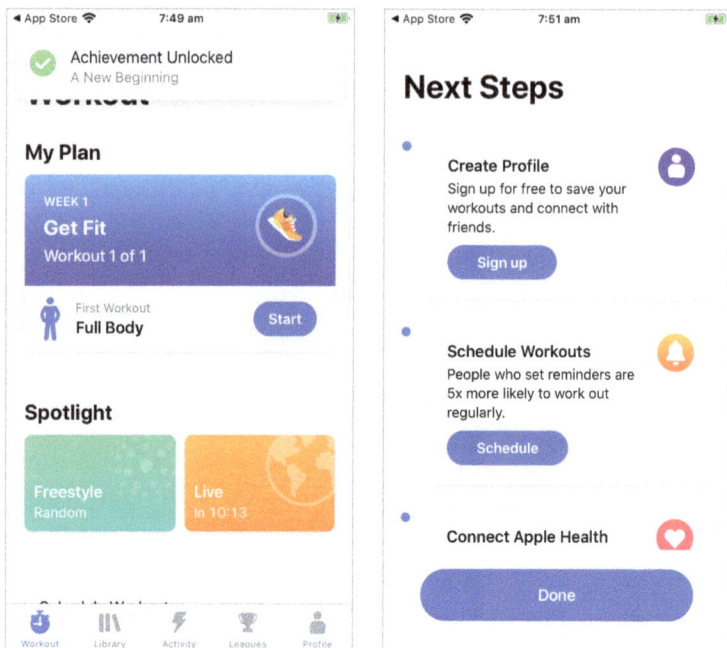

FIG 4.14: After a new user sets up their workout plan, Seven shows the populated state of their home screen, with a workout ready to go (left). Meanwhile, after the user completes their first workout, next steps are listed more explicitly, exposing prompts for scheduling workouts or creating a profile (right).

association. An incomplete "setup" checklist has persisted on my phone service account page for years, since it includes signing up for a rewards program I don't want.

Reserve the use of checklists for actions that are truly related to and part of a larger process, where it can be reasonably expected that people will eventually complete all of them, and don't leave them hanging over people's heads if they might not be completed within a reasonable timeframe. While the Seven app suggests next steps at the end of the first workout, it limits the display to that first use only and chooses the three most effective things a new user might reasonably do. And, after that workout, those prompts are split out across other key contexts in the app.

- **Don't create a superficial system of rewards.** Sometimes people try to encourage their users to take the next steps in an experience by "gamifying" it with rewards. But reward systems are complex and must be well integrated into your entire product strategy, not just used as a mechanism for new users. The rewards system itself is a whole concept you need to spend at least some part of your onboarding experience familiarizing people with, otherwise they'll be surprised by a sudden influx of rewards.

  I once installed a reading app for PDF documents, and it automatically assigned reading goals to new users. Soon, I was getting a "Congratulations" notification every time I read five pages of a technical PDF. Suffice it to say, it didn't get me to read more PDFs, but it did get me to turn off notifications. So, before you decide whether this is the right thing for you to do, first ensure that rewards are a meaningful enough part of your product to introduce as part of its onboarding experience.

- **Don't launch straight into additional flows.** Once users have truly finished a key action, they should see the fruits of their labor. If, at the end of one onboarding action, you immediately progress the user into the flows of other onboarding actions without a break, you can turn a meaningful onboarding experience into an endless slog. These tacked-on flows diminish the benefit of any signposting used in the previous action, detract from a sense of progress, and make a new user wonder, "Am I there yet?"

The follow-up state of an onboarding action closes out the loop created by the prompt and work of the action, to lead people to next steps. And this structure works not just for actions that are done just once, but those that can be done many times.

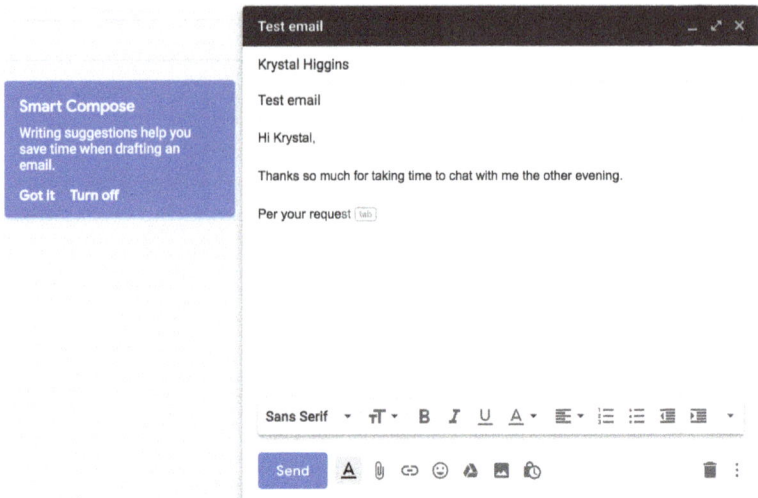

FIG 4.15: When Gmail introduced a feature called Smart Compose, a message appeared to the side of the compose screen, and text hints appeared inline with the user's typing.

REPEATABLE ACTIONS

One-time actions with the goal of setting users up will often be optimized for new users who are likely unfamiliar with the product. But when we're guiding people through repeatable actions, especially actions we want them to take routinely, we have to think with scale in mind. Repeatable actions will become too tedious if they continually subject existing users to a flow optimized only for first-time users.

If we are confident an action will only be performed on a user's first time through, we can include additional guidance that will be removed upon subsequent visits. This is not unlike when builders add scaffolding to a facade to support them as they work, then take that scaffolding away when the work is done.

When Google introduced the Smart Compose feature for Gmail, it provided such scaffolding (**FIG 4.15**). As a supplemental email writing feature, Smart Compose was introduced to

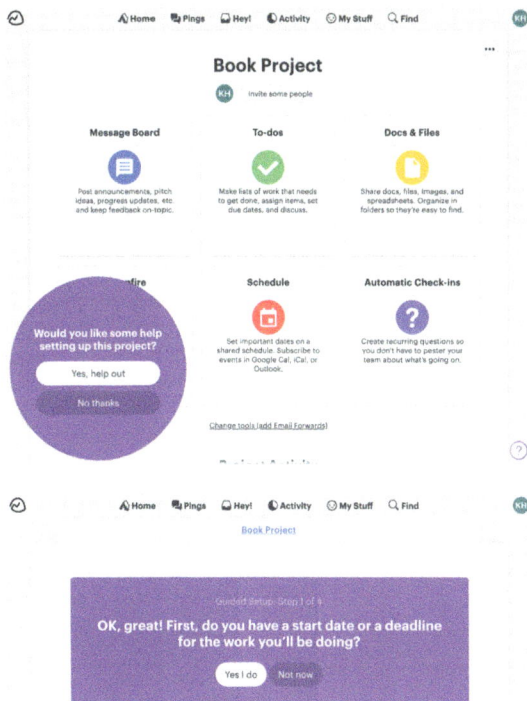

FIG 4.16: Basecamp Personal offers a sequenced project setup structure to anyone who creates a new project.

users by a special message that appeared alongside the email compose view and a visual "tab" hint that prompted the writer to accept a piece of suggested text by hitting the tab key. Upon subsequent uses, the introductory message and hint disappeared, leaving only inline text suggestions.

If we don't have a way to know for sure whether a user who is going through a repeatable action is doing it for the first time or the hundredth time, we need to plan other options. We certainly don't want everyone getting hit with introductory guidance when they don't need it! Basecamp Personal's approach for providing guidance for its repeatable action of creating a new project shows a great middle ground. They offer a sequenced flow for setting up a new project to everyone, so it doesn't matter if the user is a new or existing one. The choice to be guided is put in their hands. (**FIG 4.16**).

For many other actions where a linear structure just doesn't make sense, we should find ways to bake guidance into the flow of that action in a way that can help new users without adding extra work, noise, or extraneous structure that would frustrate existing users. We'll want a good underlying design that guides users anyway, because that will help us reinforce any behaviors or concepts we introduced later on.

REINFORCING GUIDANCE

Most actions that are part of our onboarding experience will introduce new users to concepts or activities we want them to remember or repeat. We should bear in mind that it takes more than a single encounter for users to remember key concepts or to establish a routine.

In the 1880s, German psychologist Hermann Ebbinghaus ran a series of experiments on himself to test memory and information retention. The results led him to hypothesize that our ability to remember new information drops off sharply within a day from learning it [4]. Luckily, later researchers found that the amount of information we forget can be reduced through repeated exposure to the same information, distributed at intervals over time. In the teaching world, this is called *spaced repetition* [5].

The concept of spaced repetition has been heavily researched, with strategies for implementing it based on classroom-oriented uses that don't translate 1:1 to the product world. But what we in the product world can apply is the strategy of *reinforcing* key concepts and actions over time to increase comprehension and improve routine-building. While no onboarding experience can guarantee people will remember everything they've done, reinforcement can help increase the odds of it.

Reinforcement moves us away from a set-it-and-forget it mentality and into one of building resilient guidance. It can prevent new users from encountering surprises later on, and can provide people with contextually relevant reminders that build good behaviors. Reinforcement is not about mindless repetition, but finding the contextual moments when we need to reiterate key points.

Imagine a social media app with a code of conduct established to build a sustainable, welcoming community. Certainly, one approach is to have all new users agree to the code of conduct once, the moment they first arrive. But this risks that they never read it, or skim it once and then forget. But we could reinforce that code if we referenced it again during other actions:

- A summary of the code might be displayed as a sticky post in the primary view of the app, visible while the user is browsing other posts.
- Comment fields could be accompanied by relevant code of conduct snippets about replying to other people's content.
- For new posts, the composition view could be accompanied by the snippets of the code that relate to creating content.
- We might moderate what a person has composed before it's posted, and clearly explain any code violations and how to fix them.

Each of these moments would re-emphasize the code of conduct in a way that fits the action the user is participating in, increasing the odds that it will be adopted. (And if you *can't* find reasonable, contextually relevant places to remind users of something you want to show at first run? Then maybe it's not as important as you think it is!)

BREAKING THINGS DOWN TO FIT THEM TOGETHER

Guiding users through the important actions of their onboarding journeys means thinking about it across the whole flow of the action, making it easier to reinforce important concepts or behaviors. Guidance for an action is best applied by aligning it to the three segments of an action: its prompt, its work, and its follow-up.

Together with mapping the onboarding journey, we've seen how guidance can introduce new users to the key actions of our products and guide them through completing each action successfully. While I recommend working on multiple onboarding actions at once, this per-action-focused approach can also work if your team can only tackle one action at a time. And if you don't have any onboarding actions prioritized quite yet, you can even try out this structure on any old action in your product to see if you have opportunities to improve guidance for existing users.

Up to this point in the book, you've seen a variety of examples that have hinted at different ways guidance can appear. So now that we've worked through how to structure guidance at the individual action level, let's look at the different ways we can present it.

5 PRESENTING GUIDANCE

I WAS ONCE ASKED if a "shallow" product even needs an onboarding experience. It was from a person who worked on a website for an emergency services provider, and they were curious if they needed to care about onboarding. As they put it, the goal was to get users in and out of the site as quickly as possible, so wouldn't an onboarding experience just be a frustrating waste of time?

This person was asking because their mental image of onboarding was based on other products, so they thought onboarding was limited to a particular type of pattern, like a tooltip tour. They were concerned about implementing such "onboarding" for its own sake. And that's a real concern, because focusing on one pattern as a funnel for guidance is risky.

Take Clippy, for example. Clippy was an anthropomorphic paperclip character that appeared in older versions of Microsoft Word. It would pop up in a corner of the screen and make suggestions through conversational speech bubbles. At the time, this was the product's primary channel for guiding users.

Yet the suggestions that Clippy provided grew irksome for those who continued using the product. As James Fallows summarized for the *Atlantic*, Clippy was novel and helpful *maybe* on first use, but "the next billion times you typed 'Dear...' and saw Clippy pop up, you wanted to scream" [1]. While Clippy certainly had a time and a place, it wasn't suited to being the constant channel for providing guidance.

As tempting as it sounds, there isn't one set-it-and-forget-it, one-size-fits all method for presenting guidance to new users; it just doesn't fit the reality that our products are used by people in a variety of situations, or the different contexts in which our onboarding actions might appear. The context of an action affects what kind of guidance will be appropriate and useful.

Let's get an overview of different ways we can present guidance, so that you can choose the right one for your onboarding actions. We'll start by looking at some of the elements of your product's design that can inherently provide guidance.

PRODUCT DESIGN

Consider the idea of users in a distressing situation coming to an emergency services website for the first time to figure out their next best course of action. Clearly, you'd want to avoid a distracting tutorial or tour; people are arriving in varying states of distress. The site would need to quickly guide those who were truly in an emergency toward support, and guide those in less-critical situations to non-urgent resources. Onboarding would be present in the inherent structure, layout, copy, and content of such a site, which can lead people in different situations to an ultimately positive outcome—perhaps even to the point where they'd return if they or a loved one should experience a crisis again (**FIG 5.1**).

Everybody has an onboarding experience, and it begins in the very fabric of your product's design. This is what remains should a new user skip, ignore, or forget something provided during their first experiences. It's also there to benefit new and existing users alike, since there are other moments in the user

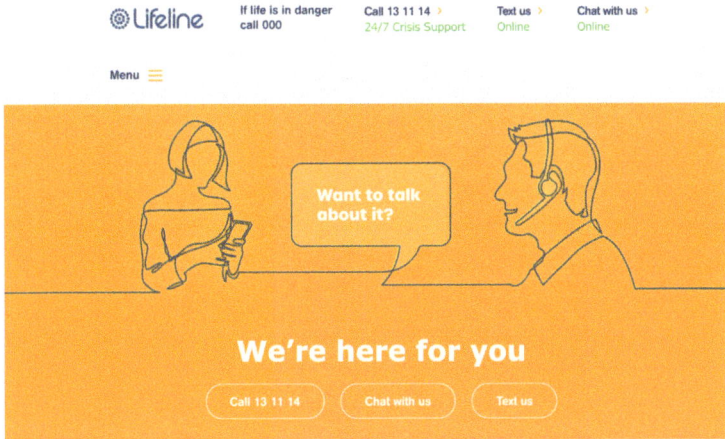

FIG 5.1: The Lifeline Australia site implicitly onboards new users to its different crisis support options by clearly placing access points in the header.

experience when people can use support, ranging from product redesigns, to new feature introductions, to people who return from a lapse. Even the most well-crafted tours and tutorials can't make up for a poorly designed product.

Be aware of how the following aspects of your product can inherently guide your users before you start implementing lots of fancy UI patterns.

Affordances

Affordances are the properties of an object that help people understand how to use it. For example, a common affordance on a website is the underlined treatment of a text link, while a common affordance for an audio assistant device is a pulsing light to indicate readiness for a command. Affordances can be powerful pieces of guidance when used carefully. I've adapted Don Norman's key qualities of affordances for how they affect guidance for new users [2]:

- **Affordances are based on conventions.** Good affordances build off existing conventions, like familiar link treatments. Adhering to the affordances that people are familiar with can encourage users to quickly take action, saving you valuable onboarding time so you don't have to teach people what things are. Avoid creating new affordances if there are already standardized ones you can use for your product, because it takes a *long* time for affordances to become a convention. Save the creation of new affordances for when you're designing a truly novel interaction.
- **Affordances have clear labels.** Labels associated with an element indicate what actions an affordance can do and reinforce actionability if it isn't recognized by some groups of users. A label that contains a verb, such as "Sign up," can indicate action, while labels containing only nouns, like "My account," may signify navigation instead. The design of buttons in a digital experience, where a label is surrounded by a container and an outline, is based on a standardized affordance.
- **Affordances use metaphors carefully.** Metaphors help people recognize a new type of affordance by connecting it to an established one from another medium. For example, a common metaphor used in writing software is to underline incorrectly spelled words in red, emulating editing marks used in the days of pen and paper (**FIG 5.2**). Red underlines are now a cue that users should tap or click the word to get a corrected spelling.

    However, use metaphors cautiously, because they can backfire. Consider Microsoft Bob, an interface for the Windows 3.1 operating system (**FIG 5.3**). An illustration of a living room served as an interactive metaphor for the user's file directory; objects in the room represented different computer tasks, such as a hanging calendar that would launch the calendar application. It didn't catch on; it was difficult for users to associate the stylized living room objects with computer tasks, and the metaphor of a brightly colored interior space felt too novice and game-like for the professional tasks people wanted to use it for [3].

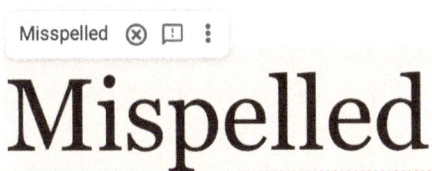

FIG 5.2: The metaphor of an editor's error mark on a misspelled word encourages interacting with the word to understand the error and see suggested replacements (example from Google Docs).

FIG 5.3: Microsoft Bob leveraged the visual metaphor of a room and its objects to present access points to a computer's file directory. Image used with permission from Microsoft and sourced from Technologizer (www.technologizer.com/2010/03/29/microsoft-bob).

- **Affordances adhere to the same conceptual model.** Use the same affordance to represent the same kinds of actions across your experience, so that people don't have to keep re-learning.

Information architecture

At the core of a product is its information architecture. *Information architecture* (IA) is the practice of organizing and structuring things to make them understandable. It is one of the biggest contributors to building and reinforcing a user's mental models, so it needs to reflect the experiences people have previously encountered.

How you group the contents of your product and how you label things can establish and reinforce mental models. These should reflect the words and groupings newcomers are already used to.

Navigation allows users to move through our content using links and search. Primary navigation should elevate the most important paths to take in a product and emphasize them over options that take people down unrelated ones. Navigation can also enable a user-led experience by offering multiple entry points to a single place.

Like in taxonomies and labels, take advantage of known navigation paradigms where possible so people don't have to learn a new way of getting around. Applying consistent UI layouts and styles across a product helps support navigation as well, because it helps new users understand the kinds of content sections they encounter across your product. If layouts and styles change across every section of your product, new users may question if they're on the right track or accidentally enter the wrong parts of your product.

Hierarchy is how we arrange and emphasize the content and elements of our product by order of their importance. What we emphasize may change as the user makes progress; for example, we may emphasize elements that encourage users to create an account, then emphasize other kinds of content once they're signed in.

Microcopy

Microcopy—the words you use across an interface to set expectations, make actionable labels, and provide continuity across flows and actions—has a lasting impact on a new user's ability to trust and understand your product. Microcopy is informed by tone of voice, the way a personality of a product is embodied. Having a consistent, appropriate tone of voice is an important part of establishing trust with new users. A banking platform that uses clear, accessible language comes across as a place that prioritizes the savings of the average person, for example; a bank that uses financially technical words and a stuffy tone does not.

Animations

The core animations we build into our product help new users understand the cause-and-effect relationship between things, know where they are in the experience, and feel a sense of progress. Transitions between states can help users know if they're moving forward or backward, and other animations can imply content location. For example, an animation that shows an item moving into a cart icon in an ecommerce app shows users where they can go to complete checkout. For a deeper understanding of the contextual power of animations, check out Val Head's book, *Designing Interface Animation*, which walks you through examples of how to use animation to convey meaning to new users.

Help content

No matter how effectively we provide guidance at the right time and place, it's impossible to anticipate every individual user's needs or desires (at least with our current technology!). Your product will be more forgiving to users in a range of situations if its help content—articles, videos, a discussion forum, etc.—is integrated into your product design. Just keep in mind that the goal isn't to make new users read a FAQ to onboard themselves; that's not guided interaction! Slack collaboration software does a great job of embedding help content into their product. It has a direct message space where users can ask for assistance from its help bot, Slackbot. Slackbot can either resolve questions directly in the conversation or respond with links to articles in its help center (**FIG 5.4**). Slack offers this help content by baking it into a core piece of its product design—direct messages—instead of tucking it away somewhere separate.

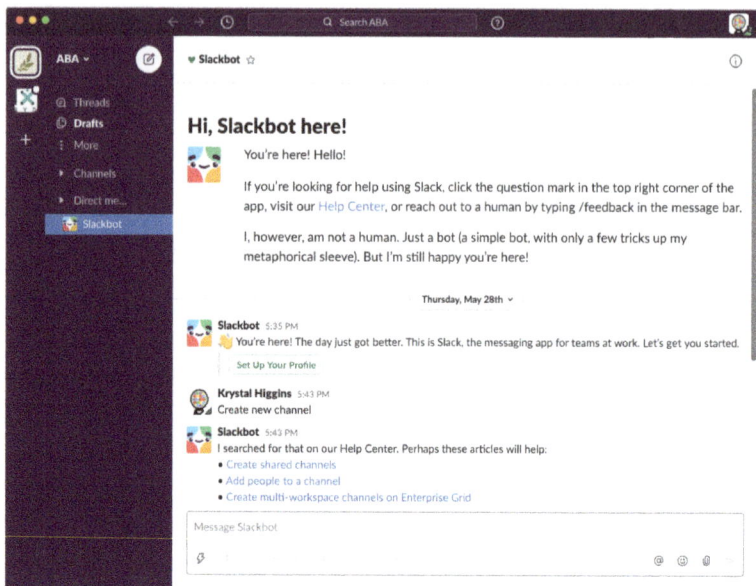

FIG 5.4: In the Slack messaging interface, a direct messaging thread with Slackbot embeds help content into the primary UI of the product, instead of making people go to an extraneous location for help.

Presets

Often, products have several settings, many of which might not make sense for new users to set up before they begin. Presets are the defaults we apply to settings, and these can make or break a user's experience since many users will stick with the ones they start with. One analysis of the configuration files of word processor software users found less than 5 percent of users changed their default settings [4].

If you choose the right presets, you set users up for success. If you choose the wrong ones, or auto-opt users into a setting they aren't comfortable with, you can create unnecessary work or break their trust. Do your research to know which presets are problematic, which presets set people up for success, and how users can become aware of or change presets.

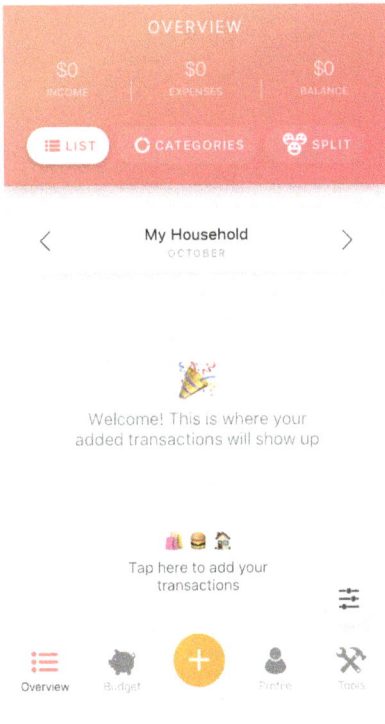

FIG 5.5: The Buddy Budget app empty state includes an embedded illustration that points to the button for adding transactions.

NOT-SO-EMPTY STATES

Some new products and features might require the user to create, add, or otherwise populate content, meaning the initial screens a user sees would be empty. Unfortunately, an empty screen doesn't really help users figure out what they should be doing. These *empty states* give you a way to provide extra guidance while keeping users in the flow and structure of your core product until the state is populated with content.

A basic version of an empty state is informative and makes obvious any actions the user can take; it doesn't describe where they should go to complete an action. Buddy Budget, a budgeting tool, uses the empty state of the user's budget space to visually direct a path to the primary navigation action where they can add their first expense (**FIG 5.5**).

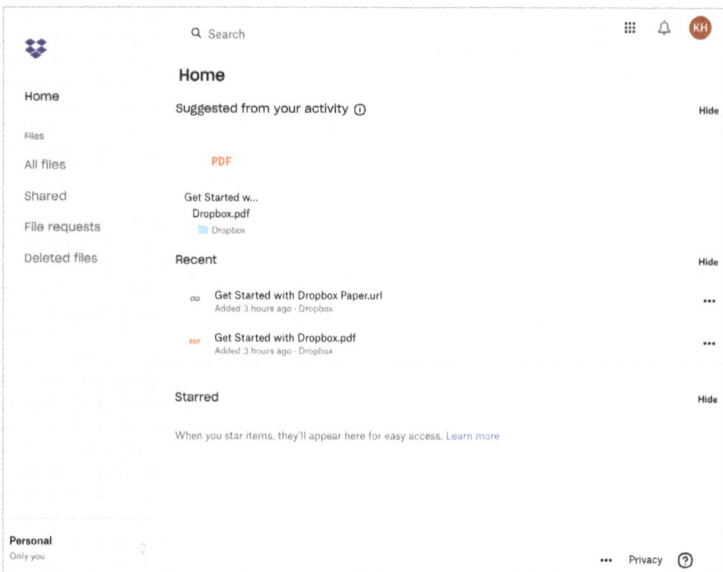

FIG 5.6: Dropbox provides an example getting started document to its empty state to give new users a preview of how files will be organized.

Empty states can also include usable, pre-populated content. Dropbox does this by both automatically adding a "Getting Started" PDF to a new user's account (**FIG 5.6**), and including a prompt to create a new document using a template.

In games, a *playthrough tutorial* is an easy and introductory level that seamlessly blends into upward levels. It's not a standalone tutorial mode, but provides an authentic, forgivable space for gameplay that lets players explore how things work at their own pace, and in their own order. Any winnings or points earned carry through to the next levels.

In products, tutorials can be a little too directive. But we can leverage an adjacent concept using what I call *playthrough content*. Playthrough content provides an interactive example, built off our product UI, that gives people a boilerplate to work from at their own speed and own pace, without being as directive as a tutorial. Notion, a workspace tool that includes

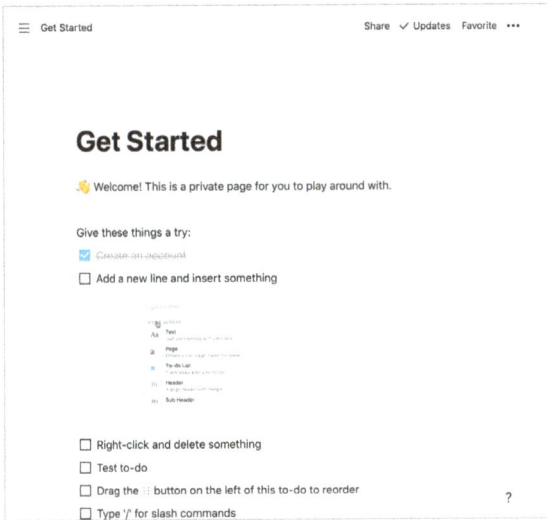

FIG 5.7: Notion's pre-made task list is ready to be edited.

FIG 5.8: Paper by WeTransfer guides new users through some drawing tools by letting them "play through" pre-made content in a demo sketchbook.

task tracking, incorporates playthrough content into its empty state. New users land on a private page pre-populated with task items which they can check off, change, or morph into their own however they'd like (**FIG 5.7**). Now that's an example of making "Let's Get Started" more actionable...and a checklist that's actually usable!

In an even more robust example of playthrough content, the iPad drawing app Paper by WeTransfer lets new users play with a demo sketchbook they've put together (**FIG 5.8**). Each page of the demo sketchbook is focused on a particular drawing feature, with an editable, pre-made drawing and a non-blocking video playing in the corner showing users how to use that feature to manipulate or complete the drawing on the page. This demo sketchbook can be returned to at any time.

ADDITIVE GUIDANCE PATTERNS

Sometimes the baseline design of our core product and its starting states are not enough to provide the guidance new users need. Or, we need temporary guidance for first-time experiences or to introduce new things. This can be a slippery slope, so I'll highlight some patterns we might augment our product design with, how they can be conducive to guided interaction, and cautions about over- and improper use. Because up-front slideshows and videos are commonly (over)used and are not conducive to guided interaction, you won't see those discussed in this chapter.

I put additive patterns we might employ for onboarding guidance into four categories, ordered here from those that appear most integrated to the most displaced:

- Inline cues
- Hints
- Overlays
- Setup wizards
- Let's look at a brief overview of these patterns, followed by some considerations.

Inline cues

Inline cues are embedded into the flow of default content and guide users to take an action related to the content they're viewing. They might present messages or banners inserted before, between, or after content, or emulate an item in a series of items.

The Trip by Skyscanner app used an inline cue inserted at the top of its screen that prompted new users to specify whether or not their current location was also their home town (**FIG 5.9**). Meanwhile, the Slack iOS app brings occasional suggestions from its Slackbot help assistant into other message channels by inserting a message from Slackbot in line with other discussions. It shows up in the flow of other content, but is clearly demarcated with a different visual treatment (**FIG 5.10**).

If we're not careful, inline cues can quickly move from being helpful insertions of guidance to irrelevant vehicles for promotion. And, the same way that people have learned to ignore ad banners on web pages (a.k.a. *banner blindness*), you'll start to train people to ignore these inline pieces of guidance in your product [5].

If using inline cues, take care to use them only occasionally during a new user's onboarding experience to provide contextually relevant prompts for action, or for temporary information that supplements the actions and options currently on screen. And, style them in a way that complements the surrounding product experience; the more you try to make them stick out from everything else, the more disjointed and advertising-like they may look.

Hints

Hints are temporary elements that highlight a piece of UI the user can act on, or to give feedback on an action just taken. Unlike an inline cue, these tend to provide less text content, since they're meant to be seen only briefly. These include patterns like:

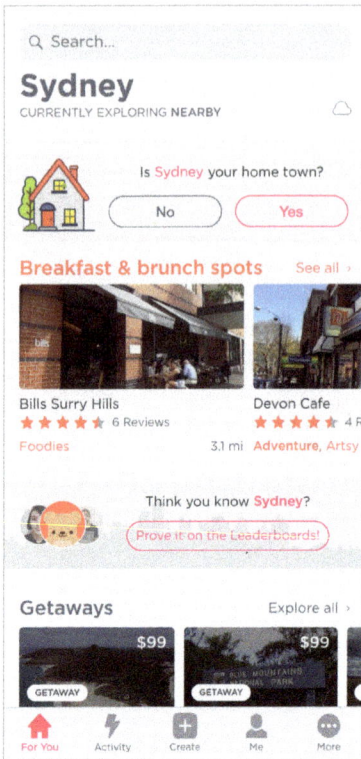

FIG 5.9: Trip by Skyscanner used inline cues around surrounding content to encourage new users to customize their experience.

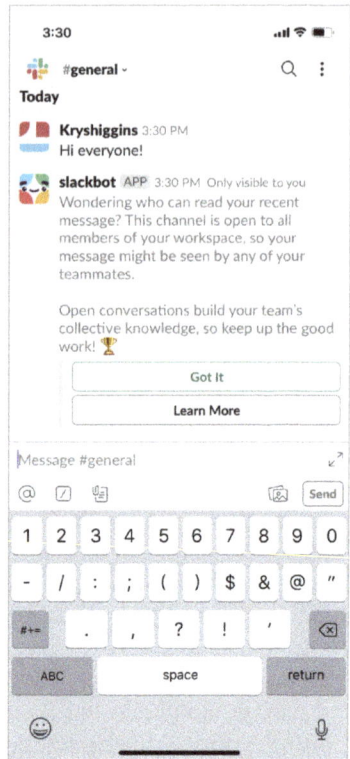

FIG 5.10: The Slack iOS app uses inline cues to insert occasional tips in line with normal conversations.

- **Highlights and badges.** Visual treatments like highlights and badges can indicate that something is interactive or has changed status. For example, a badge might appear on a new feature added to product navigation, or a thicker, colored border might be added around an object that has changed.

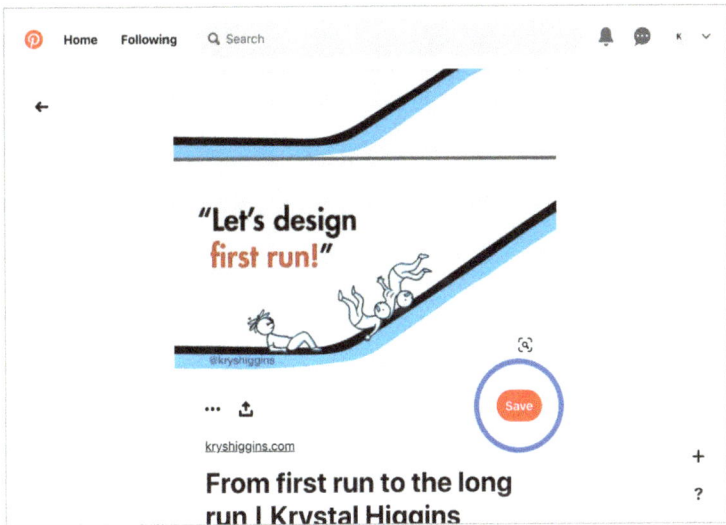

FIG 5.11: The Pinterest website uses animated emphasis in the form of a pulsing blue ring to prompt users to take action by saving a pin, which appears on their first view of the pin.

- **Animated, sonic, or haptic hints.** One-time animated, sound, or haptic hints can suggest something important is interactive or give special feedback the first time users complete a task. A visual pulse, sound, or vibration oriented around a particular piece of content might also reveal the same kind of affordance. Content curation website Pinterest PROMPTS users to save a new pin by adding a pulsing animation to the Save button (**FIG 5.11**).
- **Tooltips.** Tooltips are small informational bubbles that appear on a desktop interface when users hover over a UI element, then disappear when the cursor moves away.
- **Toasts.** Toasts are temporary messages that appear over an interface to confirm status or give feedback after a state has changed. If you use the volume key on your laptop, you may see a confirmation toast appear briefly on your screen showing the volume icon. Pinterest uses a toast to encourage users to explore similar pins after saving a pin to a board (**FIG 5.12**).

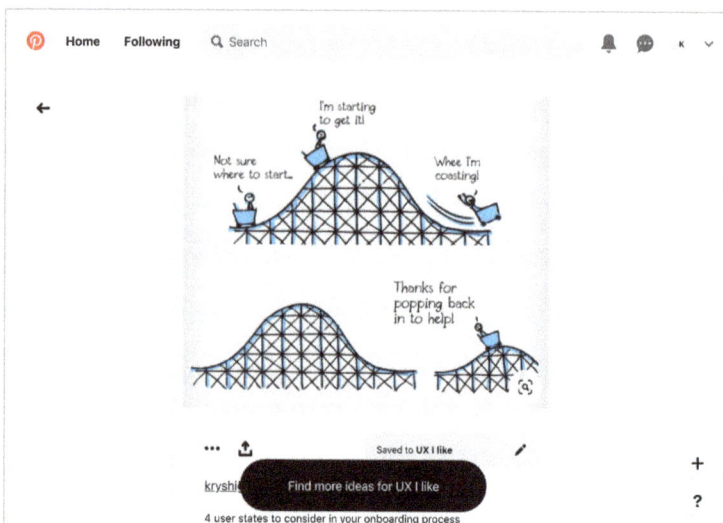

FIG 5.12: After a pin is saved on Pinterest, a toast appears to prompt the user to view similar content.

Because hints are often transient, lightweight elements, don't use them to provide important messaging or detailed information. Hints are better if you want a lightweight way to nudge users toward an optional onboarding action, to highlight a change, or to give users non-critical feedback on a completed action.

Now, with hints, we start to get into the space of UI guidance that might appear over an interface. And this brings us to...

Overlays

Overlays often pop up over your product's UI with messages and actions you can take. Overlays can be modal (putting people into a focused mode that can only be left by taking an action on the overlay) or modeless (when the overlay and underlying content can be interacted with at the same time). Unlike hints, these take up a reasonable space on a screen and typically are meant to be read or acted upon before they leave. Overlays include:

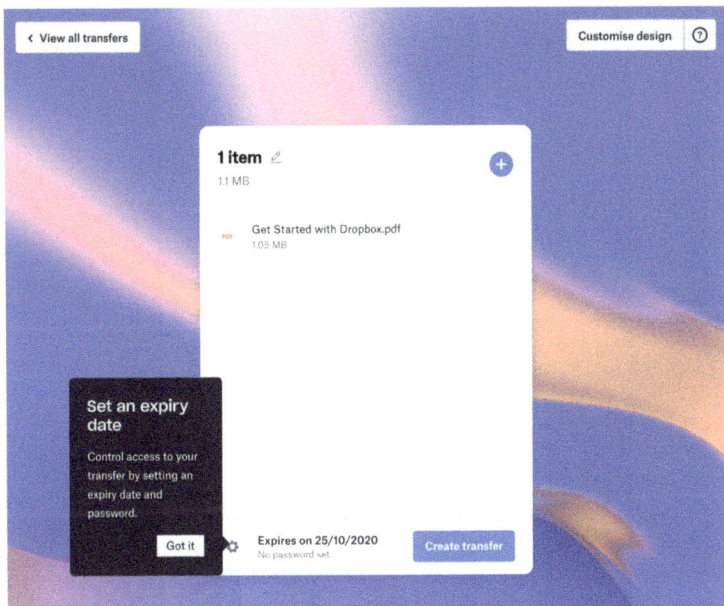

FIG 5.13: Dropbox Transfer uses the callout pattern to emphasize different subtasks of transferring a file as users move through the action for the first time.

- **Dialogs and pop-ups.** Often modal, these ask users to take action—such as pressing an OK, Cancel, or × button—to return to the underlying experience. Many device operating systems have standard dialog components that apps and sites may use, but custom dialog types can also be created.
- **Sheets.** If you've ever gone to a website that asked for consent to track browser cookies, you've probably interacted with a sheet. Sheets fix their position to the edges of the user's screen (often appearing at the top or bottom, over the underlying content).
- **Callouts.** The more prominent relatives of tooltips, callouts are message overlays that point out an element on an interface and give the user more information about them or actions they can take on them. Multiple callouts might appear as a series as part of a product tour. Dropbox Transfer uses

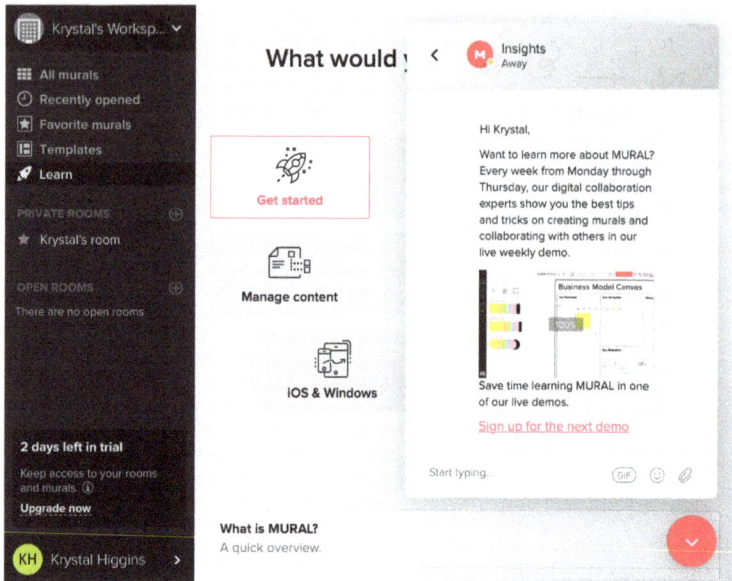

FIG 5.14: MURAL uses a floating chat bubble as an interface for making suggestions to new users or letting them ask questions.

callouts to guide people through the subtasks of transferring a file during their first use of the feature (**FIG 5.13**).

- **Floating chat bubbles.** Ah, relatively newer entrants to the world of overlays. A floating chat bubble is a chat messaging container that anchors to a corner of the user's screen. It's connected to customer service agents or bots that pop up messages to greet new users or ask if they need help. For example, virtual workspace tool MURAL displays a floating chat bubble on a user's project page to proactively suggest activities beneficial for new users, supplementing other support content (**FIG 5.14**).

Overlays especially appeal to product teams because they're displaced from the core product UI, making it easier to throw something in on short notice. But it's exactly *because* they are separate from the core interface that increases the risk of detracting from guided interaction.

There are two significant issues with overlays:

- **Interruptions push people away.** Ever walk into a store and immediately get approached by a staff member asking how they can help before you've even looked at something? When improperly applied, additive UI, particularly overlays, are the digital equivalents. For guided interaction to be successful, we can't get in the way of people actually interacting! While interrupting someone seems like a surefire way to get their attention, it can actually push them further away from the help you're trying to provide.

  When researchers from Brigham Young University partnered with engineers on the Google Chrome team to see how people interacted with security dialogs, they designed security messages to pop up during a range of activities [6]. The majority of participants ignored the content of the security messages that popped up during these tasks, illustrating how hard it can be to get people to heed important messages when presented in a disruptive way. This tendency to discard, skip, or otherwise ignore disruptions can extend to any kind of overlay users perceive to be in the way of the thing they're trying to accomplish.

- **Overlays often collide.** The more we use overlays in our product, the more we risk multiple overlays appearing on top of each other at the same time. Collisions happen when multiple overlays are prompted simultaneously or appear in rapid sequence. A collision can also occur if you have an overlay pop up to provide a message that is also visible on top of another piece of additive UI with the same message—such as an inline cue. We talked about reinforcement earlier, but what we *don't* want is this kind of mindless repetition! While collisions can happen with elements beyond overlays, they are more common in overlays because they are displaced.

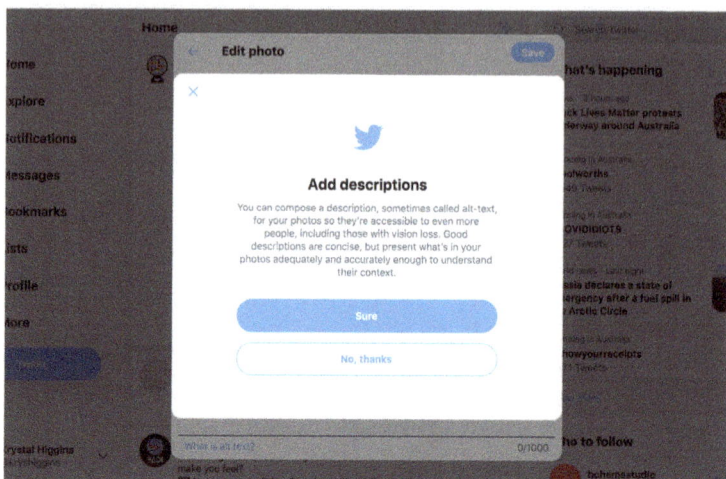

FIG 5.15: Twitter shows an informational overlay about adding alt text reactively, instead of proactively, when users chose the "Alt text" option for the first time.

What's the solution? Certainly, we should limit our use of overlays, or even avoid using them. But they can be useful for delivering content, messages, and deep-diving into a focused action…if we show them at a time that respects the user's situation.

The best times to display an overlay tend to be during a natural pause in a user's experience (as found in the aforementioned security dialog study), or in direct response to user action. For example, Twitter uses an informational dialog to introduce alt text for images (**FIG 5.15**). The dialog appears to new users after they select the "Alt text" option on an image for the first time; it only appears again if the user clicks a "What is alt text?" help link.

Meanwhile, Caviar, a food delivery app, uses a dialog to prompt users to enable notifications, but only as the follow-up to placing their first order. This contextually frames the prompt around order status updates, making it more relevant to users in the moment (**FIG 5.16**).

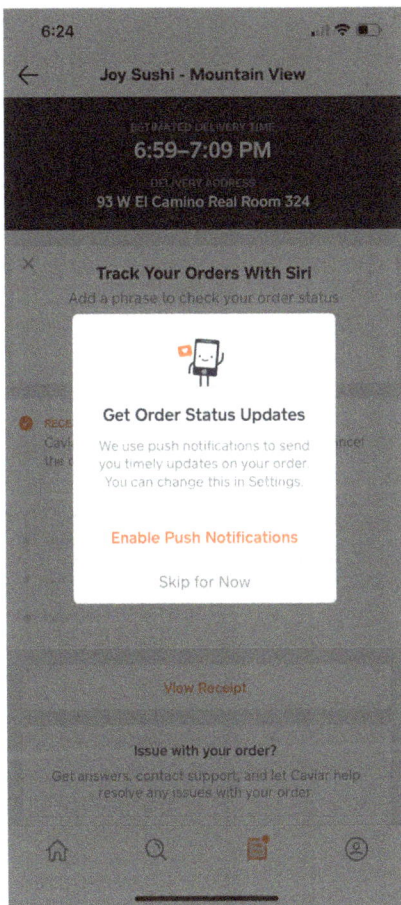

FIG 5.16: Caviar, a food delivery app, shows a dialog asking users to enable notifications after ordering their first meal.

Essentially, you want to reduce the number of overlays that push themselves in front of the user when they're in the middle of a task. Save that proactive behavior for critical issues or updates that materially affect the user. If you use an overlay, opt instead to display them responsively as the user interacts. For example, a floating chat bubble could be quite disruptive, but one that only shows a message when the user taps on an icon is much more reasonable.

Setup wizards

In the previous chapter, we touched on how people might be guided through an onboarding action through sequencing. While there are several formats for providing that sequence, a *wizard* is a particularly common, standalone pattern for presenting the subtasks of an onboarding action as a series of individual screens, applying a consistent layout of imagery, text, progress indicators, and buttons across them.

It's important we understand what makes an appropriate use of a wizard pattern distinct from a slideshow pattern in disguise (since that's also a series of screens!). A wizard can be effective as long as:

- it's applied only to a well-scoped onboarding action,
- the action represents only a one-time setup or otherwise complex and infrequently visited flow, and
- each screen of the wizard is focused on getting the user to take an action, not acting as a surface to serve up pure information.

In the version of Wear OS by Google I worked on, the mobile app setup flow used a standardized wizard layout for all of its steps, where imagery was at the top, text following below, and buttons for going back or taking action at the bottom (**FIG 5.17**). We also saw other examples of wizards from products shown in the last chapter, like Basecamp and Airtasker.

Not all products should use a wizard for presenting guidance; while wizards include some interaction, they can easily make an action feel more complex or tedious than it needs to be. They can also give people the feeling you're interrupting their experience, just like overlays do, because they obfuscate the product they're serving.

FIG 5.17: The setup wizard for an early version of Wear OS by Google used a consistent layout of imagery, text, and actions across all screens.

Enable Bluetooth sharing

Your phone needs Bluetooth sharing enabled to
communicate with your watch.

BACK   ENABLE

EMAILS AND OTHER CHANNELS

Not all guidance that encourages users to take their next steps in an onboarding journey needs to, or realistically can, be presented in product. Emails and notifications are two of the most common alternate channels for providing guidance to new users after their first use of a product.

For some organizations, such as nonprofits, emails may be the only way to onboard someone to the bigger cause or after their initial interaction. Emails are also touted as important channels for guidance in SAAS products. And while following these kinds of organizations on social media might provide an ongoing channel to provide broad updates, emails can provide content more tailored to a user's current state in a product.

FIG 5.18: Video streaming service Stan sends a welcome email after someone signs up for a free trial with a single next step: to "Watch Now."

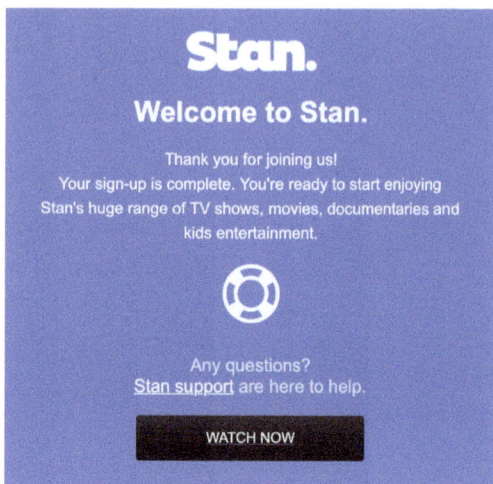

However, onboarding emails can easily run away with us if we're not careful. It's very easy for someone to unsubscribe or mark your emails as spam if they get annoyed. These considerations need to be part of a holistic email and content strategy for your product—now, that's a whole other book, but here are a few best practices specifically when considering emails as part of your onboarding strategy:

- **Do send a welcome message shortly after users provide their email address.** Be brief and action-oriented instead of simply informing users about your product, providing one to three actionable next steps they can take. When users sign up for a free trial of video streaming service Stan, they receive a confirmation email with their trial start/end dates and a "start watching" action they can take as a next step (**FIG 5.18**).
- **Don't send additional onboarding emails without disclosing that you'll do so.** If a user is providing an email during signup, checkout, or subscription, give notice that you'll be sending out emails and give them the option to unsubscribe. The latter may even be a legal requirement in some countries!

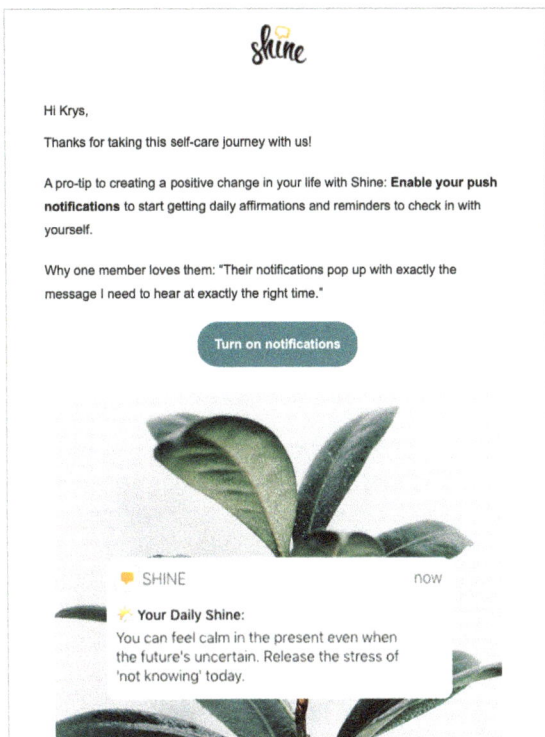

FIG 5.19: Mindfulness app Shine sends a contextually-relevant onboarding prompt via email after several days if a new user hasn't yet enabled reminders for their daily affirmations.

- **Do send additional onboarding emails that reflect recent user activities.** There are many email services that let you send onboarding emails on a prescribed schedule, but these can appear irrelevant to users who don't follow your prescribed schedule. I recently experienced this while using the mindfulness app Shine. Seven days after I set up a daily self-reflection schedule, I received an email suggesting I enable push notifications to get reminders to do my check-ins (**FIG 5.19**). The simple logic used to check whether notifications were enabled before sending this reminder made the email relevant to me. If I already had notifications turned on and received that email, I would feel like the product was baselessly pestering me.

- **Don't confuse onboarding emails with marketing emails.**
  Nothing will dilute your onboarding emails more than
  weekly (or worse, daily) emails about promotions, new features, and other products unrelated to their journey as a
  new user. Make sure they can be successful in your product
  first! Only request someone's email address if it's relevant to
  what they're doing. The ProPublica example from the last
  chapter, which used an inline prompt for email provision,
  is a good example of requesting that information without
  interrupting the user.

Notifications

For apps and the web browsers that support them, push notifications can provide timely messages if people aren't in your
product, but still have the app or are on your webpage. They
can be used to keep new users engaged in the actions you want
to build up as a routine, or to call attention to something that
can help them. For example, the Buddy Budget app sends an
initial notification to new users of its mobile app suggesting that
a new user download the desktop application as a companion
experience. The notification is immediately actionable.

Because people get a lot of notifications throughout the day,
ensure they represent actionable content, and avoid using these
for purely informational messages like welcome notifications.
Like emails, push notifications are best when they're immediately actionable and tied to recent activity in your product.

Text messages

Increasingly, a number of mobile applications are leveraging
text messages to send new users welcome messages and tips,
since they can be certain they'll reach users on the same mobile
device via a phone number. Unfortunately, text messages share
the negative aspects of both push notifications (they're disruptive), and email (they don't offer space to elaborate, and
links may be seen as spam)—*and* they can eat up users' mes-

saging allowance. An initial welcome text or very occasional promo text might be worth looking into if you don't have access to a user's email account, but don't rely on this as a channel for onboarding.

EVERYTHING WORKS TOGETHER

This chapter covered the different ways we might present guidance to new users through product design; starting states; additive UI patterns, such as inline cues, hints, and overlays; and other messaging channels, like emails and notifications. While not exhaustive, this list is meant to show onboarding isn't embodied by a single slideshow or video, but rather may be presented in any manner that best fits the kind of action a new user has encountered and the context they're in. We can use different sets of approaches as long as we think about how they can all work together.

Consider how some new devices arrive: wrapped in a clear plastic marked with descriptions of what the device's parts visible under the plastic do. But what happens when someone inevitably peels off that plastic and throws it away? We must make sure we aren't just putting in throwaway guidance when we decide how to present that guidance to our users. In fact, we should be thinking about how we can use different methods that seamlessly connect to each other. *Multimodal interfaces* allow users to interact with an interface in more than one way to make an experience friendlier for them. We can use a multimodal approach to provide guidance as well, as long as we keep the following in mind:

- **Your product's baseline design is the foundation for all your guidance.** The more you can bake onboarding into your core experience, the more resilient your guidance will be in different situations.
- **Use additive UI patterns** if you need specialized support for new actions or to reinforce a core concept. Start by looking at less disruptive additions like inline cues and hints. Con-

sider overlays only when they're respectful of the user's situation and won't result in messy collisions or interruptions.

- **Add supplementary guidance in other channels**, such as emails or notifications. Keep in mind that people may unsubscribe from these at any time.

Once you understand how you'll provide the guidance you need for your new users, you're ready to scale your guidance for long-term benefit.

6 SCALING GUIDANCE

AT THIS POINT, we've worked through the pieces that make up a guided interaction strategy for user onboarding. We've gotten ready for new users by getting our team on board and clearing first-run roadblocks, we've mapped onboarding journeys, we've broken down the actions that make up a journey, and we've learned what types of guidance we might use to support them. The result is guidance that is woven into a new user's interaction with the product.

So we're all set, right?

Not quite. Our audiences will, ideally, continue to scale in size, but likely also in breadth. Our products will change, either adding, removing, or redesigning features. Just like audiences and products evolve, so too will user onboarding and the guidance that makes it up. We can't guide new users if we treat our onboarding experience as something to be built and maintained in isolation from other features. To set your future new users up for success, let's look at a few considerations for embedding guided interaction in your product design process, and how it can scale its impact over time.

MANAGING GUIDED INTERACTION

We need to ensure the processes we use to design guidance for our new users, and the decisions we've made along the way, are incorporated into our core design process. This way, we'll be better prepared to make sure everything launches properly and to make adjustments over time.

Document decisions

Documenting the main decisions from the onboarding journey map activity in Chapter 3 in a text document will give you a dedicated space to capture core use definitions, core use routines, entry situations, and a list of prioritized onboarding actions (**FIG 6.1**). This document can be used as a jumping off point for all related resources, like the visual onboarding map, the research that fed into the prioritized list of onboarding actions, the specific designs for each onboarding action, the product requirements documents, or the specific tasks in any kind of project management tool you might be using.

Put guided interaction into action

Once you've organized your decisions and designs, figure out the best way to integrate the work into your product development process. In an ideal world, we would implement all the guidance we identified for our user onboarding journey all at once; that will certainly prevent too many things from being out of sync and give users maximum benefit! But even when you have a shortlist of prioritized onboarding actions designed and ready to go, it might be too much work to get everyone to commit to doing it all at once.

Don't let that stop you from introducing guided interaction to your product development process. I encourage you to break down how your team will tackle the work, just like how you break down the work of onboarding for new users!

Here are some ways to put guided interaction into action in your development process:

Core use state:	Sells 10+ items/week; has high seller rating
Core use routines:	· Maintains a storefront · Responds to buyers within 24 hours · Checks top selling trends every month · Lists more than five items per week · Shares items they're selling on social media · Ships purchases within two days using quality packaging
Entry situation 1:	Wants to get rid of clutter; searches internet for places that will sell similar items
Prioritized onboarding actions:	· Views results for similar items · Copies details from similar item · Creates an account · Posts first item for sale · Downloads mobile app · Turns on mobile seller notifications · Ships sold item · Connects social media account · Creates item templates
Entry situation 2:	Wants to set up a store; receives a referral link from a peer
Prioritized on-boarding actions:	· Redeems free trial · Customizes preset shop theme · Posts first item for sale · Creates an account · Converts to subscription · Sets up basic seller profile · Enables shop notifications · Creates item templates · Connects social media account · Subscribes to weekly trends newsletter

FIG 6.1: This table shows one way to document and organize core use definition, entry situations, routines, and the prioritized key actions that come out of onboarding journey mapping.

- **Start making core product design adjustments in existing flows** that research has shown are problematic for new or existing users, like swapping out confusing terms with simple ones, or making sure certain words or images are used consistently. This will introduce your team to the idea that guidance can be woven into your core product experience.
- **Identify and remove instances of poorly performing front-loaded instruction or displaced guidance**, like slideshows or overlays, that your research or metrics show are not adding significant value. This will clear the stage for adding guided interaction and relieve your team from maintaining an extra piece of UI that might not be helpful. If your team is not comfortable doing this, you could set up an A/B experiment to measure the effects of removing the element as compared to keeping it.
- **Use your onboarding documentation as a rollout guide for launching designs for each onboarding action**, addressing those actions that tend to occur earlier in a new user's onboarding journey or those that were at the very top of the prioritized list of actions. To do this well, ensure the next steps of an implemented onboarding action don't point to an action that doesn't exist yet, and assign specific rollout dates to each action to make sure you don't launch one and forget about the others.

Evaluate and iterate

As you start building out and launching an onboarding experience, keep tabs on it so you can iterate, as needed, over time. Here are a few tactics I recommend to get a comprehensive pulse check on your onboarding design:

- **Diary studies** allow you to observe how and why a user does or doesn't progress through your product over a period of weeks. You could compare a "before" group to an "after" group to see what happens after you add or change your onboarding guidance.

- **Cohort analysis** gives you data at scale about actions new users do or don't take. Use logging to track actions in your product, then compare and contrast what groups of users (cohorts) do over a time period to see if cohorts exhibit different behaviors after introducing, changing, or removing guidance.
- **Usability studies** test a user's ability to complete an individual action you're trying to guide them through. This won't give you a view of how successful your onboarding journey is overall, but can help you make localized changes within one action.
- **Offboarding feedback** from new users who decided to delete an account or cancel a free trial is a good way to learn what might need to change to better welcome future new users. You might find that you didn't set appropriate expectations before people sign up, or that the resulting experience was too confusing to them. While certainly not a replacement for the above methods, consider asking users who leave early on in their experience why it wasn't a good fit.

Don't get discouraged if your research reveals that some things may need to be iterated on. Applying guided interaction to your onboarding experience is like designing any other part of a product—there will always be opportunities for future improvement.

Avoid siloed onboarding

One risk with implementing onboarding design over time is that we can end up with siloed results that create a confusing experience for new users. If you work on a product that's existed for a long time, you've probably encountered problems with some parts growing inconsistent with other parts. While this doesn't mean we can't implement the guided interaction of our onboarding experience in a gradual manner, there are a few things you can do to avoid this kind of siloed sprawl.

Standardize your decisions in a pattern library

Standardizing the decisions you've made for applying guided interaction for new users can make a great addition to any pattern library or design system that your team already uses. This will ensure any guidance you use for new users and existing users all work together as part of a system of design and gives you a toolkit you can draw upon for future additions or iterations.

The GOV.UK Design System organizes onboarding patterns by the user need it addresses—rather than under "onboarding" or "first run"—so they can be considered holistically alongside other similar contexts (**FIG 6.2**) [1].

Even if you don't already have a design system or pattern library, you can start standardizing patterns by cataloging instances of guidance you use in your current product and instances of new guidance you designed when breaking down onboarding actions. Then, identify patterns that are used frequently. Check out the Resources section to learn more about designing pattern libraries and product-wide design systems.

Distribute ownership

Perhaps your team considers you the "owner" of user onboarding in your product. Perhaps you'll become the de facto owner after reading this book. But the design of guidance and user onboarding should never be owned by just one person. If it is, your team risks losing all that person's valuable knowledge if they leave. One team I worked with had a new onboarding designer every year because they were always burned out by the work, leaving the team constantly starting from scratch. As you can imagine, that can make us fall back on using poorly integrated pieces of frontloaded instruction, instead of guidance that scales for the onboarding journey.

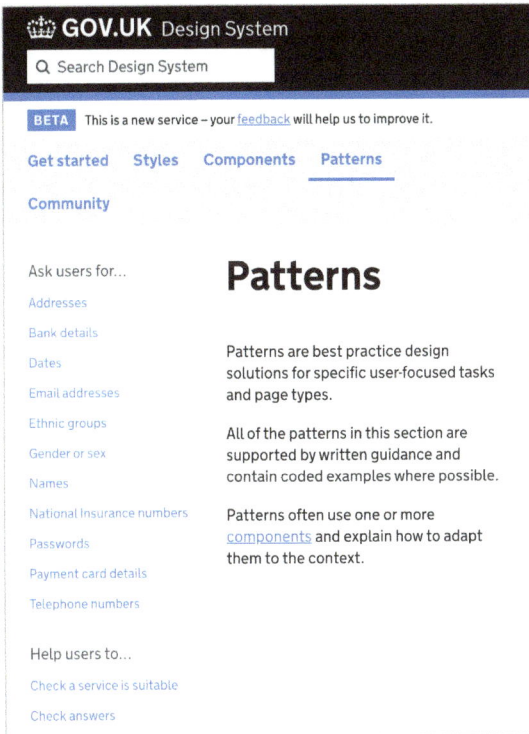

FIG 6.2: The GOV.UK Design System website organizes onboarding patterns by the user need they address, so any pattern can be leveraged for both new and existing users who may share the same need.

Making onboarding design the responsibility of the entire team will help you avoid this dilemma. The shared responsibility keeps your entire team accountable to a well-integrated onboarding experience, retains valuable knowledge on the team, and prevents the need to constantly start over. In the same way that you must let new users interact with a product to acclimate to it, involve your immediate and adjacent teams in the definition, design, and maintenance of onboarding guidance.

EXTENDING GUIDED INTERACTION

While one user's onboarding journey may end, the need to have guidance in your product doesn't. Up until now, we've looked at the application of guided interaction primarily through the lens of new user onboarding. But its benefit is not limited to the initial onboarding of new users. This approach not only helps us grow our experience around those new users as they settle in, but can help guide existing users through new situations.

Personalizing the experience

One benefit of guiding through interaction is that it gives us more time to grow our understanding of the user, their interests, and their needs as they interact with our product, so we don't need to ask for everything up front. As they use our product, we can reflect on what we've learned from the activities they've done, the content they've created, or the preferences they've set by adjusting our prompts for action.

This means exploring what the product looks like to new users, and considering how it can evolve into something more personal as they invest more time and complete more onboarding actions. For example, when a new user interacts with the Tripadvisor website, the homepage adjusts to reflect their recent searches, and displays an inline prompt to start building a trip around them (**FIG 6.3**).

New feature introductions

Guided interaction can be just as helpful for rolling out new features and functionality to established users as it is for new user onboarding. When Etsy introduced its new Pattern feature, which allows sellers to create a custom website design for their shops, they used an inline banner to prompt users to enter the experience, and applied in-context guidance for trying out their first shop design (**FIG 6.4**).

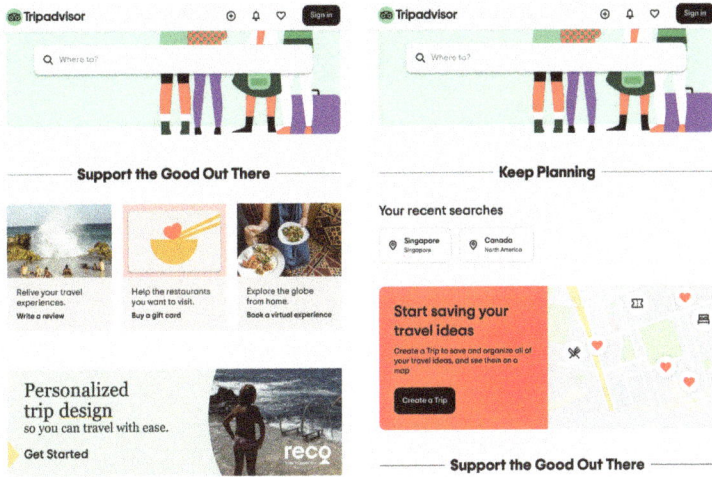

FIG 6.3: Tripadvisor's homepage displays generalized content on a user's first visit. After the user interacts with destination pages, the homepage adapts to reflect the user's potential trip planning locations.

Product or service updates

There are cases when you might need to send in-product messages to users about changes or updates. Put high-priority messages in the context of a specific, relevant interaction; for example, during the COVID-19 pandemic, many ridesharing and public transit apps used guidance at the point of looking up travel options to encourage people to stay home, and only travel if absolutely necessary (**FIG 6.5**). A one-time, first-run explanation would have been easier to forget or ignore.

Product redesigns

Occasionally, a product may be redesigned so core workflows are altered, such as an operating system update to a phone or computer. Guiding through interaction is a strategy that can help users through this change instead of just popping up an overlay or slideshow to describe features to that existing user.

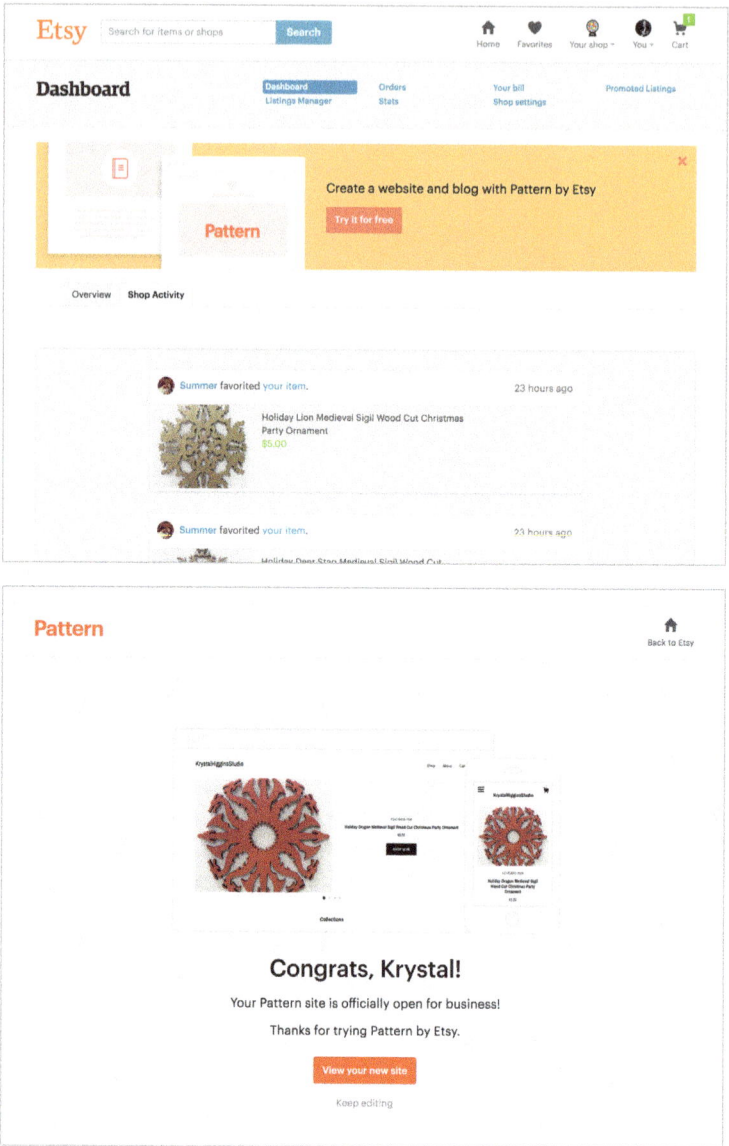

FIG 6.4: Just as in onboarding, guided interaction helped Etsy introduce their Pattern feature to existing sellers. They used an inline prompt that guided users into a free trial (top image), and a follow-up to confirm success and suggest next steps (bottom image).

FIG 6.5: Mobile app Transit showed a COVID-19 awareness message in the context of searching for nearby transit options.

For example, when the Google Drive team migrated existing Google Docs users to the newer Google Drive experience, they put guidance in the context of the existing version of the product to prime people for the impending change. They also let people opt in to the new version, and switch back and forth between versions for a time so they could learn the differences at their own pace [2].

Re-boarding lapsed users

There are also times when a user returns to a product after a period of non-use. Maybe the lapse is part of the natural usage cycle of the product, or the user left because their life circumstances required them to pause and focus elsewhere for a while. Either way, users might need to be guided through any differences between the version that exists now and the one they last used, so they can quickly pick up where they left off.

GUIDANCE FOR EVERYONE

From new user onboarding to guiding existing users through new features, changes, and lapses, a guided interaction approach will make for products that better support our users where they are. The strategies for mapping onboarding actions, breaking those actions down, and finding the right types of guidance for them can be applied to any point in your design process. They help you see your product through the perspective of a new user and help you improve how your product guides everyone.

"YOU'RE ALL SET!"

WE HAVE ARRIVED AT THE END of this book, which walked through redefining user onboarding, mapping an onboarding journey, and breaking down the work and modes by which we present guidance. We've encountered many different examples of guided interaction along the way, but I hope the core idea is clear: we create a better experience for everyone when we weave support into the context of a user's interaction with a product, instead of using a one-size-fits all piece of instruction at the beginning of the onboarding experience.

Guided interaction is a concept that sounds so simple, so intrinsic to interaction design, that it seems odd to have to write a book about it at all. But this book is a much-needed counterbalance to a mindset that sees user onboarding as something that can be reduced to a simple formula. Learning and onboarding are personal, nuanced journeys. We need to create products that welcome all sorts of new users from all sorts of situations. While it might mean we have to do a little extra work to convince our teams to shift to this integrated model, the payoff will be richer: we'll get more informed, engaged, and retained users.

So, even though you're at the end of this book, I hope you are far from being finished. My goal is that you leave this book inspired by the promise of guided interaction and ready to dive in. Embracing guided interaction means you have the power, *anywhere* in your product, to design user onboarding for the better. Whether you start by removing a piece of front-loaded instruction, redesigning one of your onboarding actions, or mapping the entire onboarding journey, you can find the right next step that's best for you.

It's time to get started.

ACKNOWLEDGMENTS

THANK YOU, READER, for journeying this book. A book that I couldn't have finished without a lot of supportive people.

First, to the editing staff, Lisa Maria, Sally, Caren, Danielle, Katel, and everyone else who turned my "organized mess" approach to writing into a well-structured book.

To Christine, Kate, Rachael, Rem, MC, Elle, Tim, and Angelique, not just for giving me helpful feedback to improve my work, but for generally lending me support that kept me going. To Christine especially, who was somehow always ready with an encouraging text or video call even on the days when I was ready to chuck my laptop out the window. To my parents, who were always supportive of my out-there goals: even though you couldn't be here for this book, it exists because of you. And cheers to Kyle for the laughs when things looked down.

To my colleagues and friends, past and present—Steve, Alanna, Dani, Randy, Rory, Brett, Jacklynn, Josh S., Thryn, Eric, John, Kenneth, LP Fam, Elissa, Cale, Daniel, Andy, and many, many more: thank you for creating space for me to talk your ears off about user onboarding for weeks, months, and years.

Thanks to all the researchers and product teams who have published findings in the onboarding space, and to all of those who have published work in areas adjacent to it. Many thanks to the experienced authors who gave me advice about writing books. And a great number of thanks to all the companies and product teams that have created products with guidance in them that help show the world what good human-centered onboarding can look like.

Finally, I want to acknowledge that this book was written during quite an era of human history. I thank all the medical professionals, teachers, and essential workers who kept people healthy, fed, and otherwise supported during a massive worldwide pandemic. I thank all the protesters who fought for, and are still fighting for, racial, environmental, and political justice across the world. The future will be a better place because of people like you.

Hearts, stars, and rainbows, everyone.

ADDITIONAL RESOURCES

USER ONBOARDING DESIGN IS not a distinct field, but a practice grounded in many educational, behavioral, human resources, and design concepts. In addition to the references made throughout the book, the following articles, blog posts, books, and tools will give you some initial ideas for diving deeper into key aspects of onboarding design.

Learning and behavior

- The concept of educational *scaffolding* embodies the idea of taking a new student from their current level of understanding to the next level until, eventually, expertise is reached. "Understanding Scaffolding and the ZPD in Educational Research" by Irina Verenikina is a good overview of educational scaffolding and the different ways it can be interpreted (core.ac.uk/download/pdf/36994249.pdf, PDF).
- We briefly touched on the Ebbinghaus forgetting curve and spaced repetition in Chapter 4. "Spaced Repetition Promotes Efficient and Effective Learning: Policy Implications for Instruction" by Sean H. K. Kang will help paint a more complete picture of how this concept can be applied in an educational context (researchgate.net/publication/290511665_Spaced_Repetition_Promotes_Efficient_and_Effective_Learning_Policy_Implications_for_Instruction, PDF).
- "The Magical Number Seven, Plus or Minus Two: Some Limits on our Capacity for Processing Information" by George Miller provides the groundwork for a concept called *chunking*, in which we break apart information so it's easier for people to remember. Just note that the "seven" part of the theory has since been debunked; chunks can be effective in different sizes (psychclassics.yorku.ca/Miller).
- The Fogg Behavioral Model, developed by behavioral scientist BJ Fogg, offers a detailed dive into the mechanics of behavior change based on the relationship between motivation, ability, and an actionable prompt (behaviormodel.org).

- "The 'IKEA Effect': When Labor Leads to Love" outlines the benefits of letting people have a hands-on role in creating something for themselves (hbs.edu/ris/Publication%20 Files/11-091.pdf). This behavior isn't limited to physical products, either, at least according to the "I designed it myself" effect (researchgate.net/publication/220534385_The_I_ Designed_It_Myself_Effect_in_Mass_Customization).
- Coglode provides a handy cheat sheet for a number of psychological concepts and their effects on user interaction (coglode.com).
- And, because some form of behavioral change is often the result of onboarding and guiding our users, it's important to understand the broader space—including its challenges and ethics. "Behavioral Design 2020 and Beyond," a collection of thoughts from many in the field, will give you a good primer (medium.com/behavior-design-hub/behavioral-design-2020-and-beyond-dc88a87f3b97).

Employee onboarding

- Some current approaches to user onboarding design are derived from the world of employee orientation. "Organizational Socialization: Its Content and Consequences" by Georgia Chao, Anne O'Leary-Kelly, Samantha Wolf, Howard Klein, and Philip Gardner was the origin point for many modern approaches (researchgate.net/publication/232462733_Organizational_Socialization_Its_Content_and_Consequences).

Product design for better onboarding

- *Growth Design* is a movement away from growth "hacking" and toward a more comprehensive, design-driven approach to healthy product growth. The video "Leading Growth-Driven Design: Levers for Sustained Growth" from Chetana Deorah will give you an introduction (youtu.be/ P7KwkXYWcpY).
- *Everyday Information Architecture* by Lisa Maria Marquis and *How to Make Sense of Any Mess* by Abby Covert are both great

resources for designing information architecture that guides users (everydayia.com, howtomakesenseofanymess.com).
- *Microinteractions* by Dan Saffer is a comprehensive guide to structuring the small, single-task actions in a product, and a deeper dive into how to break down and design actions for better impact (microinteractions.com).
- *Designing Interface Animation* by Val Head teaches you how to design animations that provide better understanding, (rosenfeldmedia.com/books/designing-interface-animation).
- To design better UI patterns, check out *Designing Interfaces: Patterns for Effective Interaction Design* by Jenifer Tidwell, Charles Brewer and Aynne Valencia (oreilly.com/library/view/designing-interfaces-3rd/9781492051954).
- For existing design systems, check out the GOV.UK Design System, Google's Material Design, and Apple's Human Interface Guidelines (design-system.service.gov.uk, m3.material.io, developer.apple.com/design/human-interface-guidelines).
- *Strategic Writing for UX* by Torrey Podmajersky breaks down tips for UX writing, including for the user onboarding phase (oreilly.com/library/view/strategic-writing-for/9781492049388).
- Since user onboarding often involves signup, learn how to design better authentication experiences with the video "Fixing the Failures of the Authentication UX" by Jared Spool (youtu.be/Jxwgoy4Itxw).
- Finally, it's worth noting that offboarding—the experience of someone leaving a product—serves as bookend to onboarding. *Ends* by Joe MacLeod offers a look at this side of the user journey (andend.co/book).

Inclusive onboarding

I strongly recommend understanding what makes products more accessible to new users so we can create products that welcome people from any situation.

- *Accessibility for Everyone* from Laura Kalbag is a practical read on applying accessibility best practices to products (laurakalbag.com/book).

- *Cross-Cultural Design* by Senongo Akpem has a structured approach to supporting multiple cultures (senongo.net/cross-cultural-design).
- The GenderMag Project website provides different personas to help you design for diverse audiences (gendermag.org).
- *Mismatch* by Kat Holmes offers a broad lens into inclusive product design (mitpress.mit.edu/9780262539487/mismatch).

Research methods

- *Just Enough Research* by Erika Hall offers an in-depth look at user research methods, which you can use to understand new users and evaluate your onboarding experience.
- *Build Better Products* by Laura Klein provides strategies for using both user research and analytics to product design (rosenfeldmedia.com/books/build-better-products).
- "Measuring the User Experience on a Large Scale: User-Centered Metrics for Web Applications" from Google Research helps us think about metrics holistically with the HEART framework (research.google/pubs/measuring-the-user-experience-on-a-large-scale-user-centered-metrics-for-web-applications).

Onboarding design tools

- Digital collaboration tools are helpful for plotting the onboarding journey of new users in collaboration with teammates. Two I've used have been Figma and MURAL (figma.com, mural.co).
- For additional resources you might use to design better user onboarding, view my blog (kryshiggins.com/onboarding).

REFERENCES

Where possible, links to non-paywalled versions have been provided. However, a link's payment and access status may change at any time.

Chapter 1 | What Is Onboarding?

1   *What is Onboarding Exactly?* https://www.peopleadmin.com/2013/01/what-is-onboarding-exactly

2   Rozin, P., & Royzman, E. B. (2001). Negativity Bias, Negativity Dominance, and Contagion. *Personality and Social Psychology Review*, 5(4), 296-320. https://doi.org/10.1207/S15327957PSPR0504_2

3   Carroll, John & Rosson, Mary Beth. (1987). Paradox of the active user. 80-111. https://www.researchgate.net/publication/262322669_Paradox_of_the_active_user

4   Joyce, Alita. (2020). *Mobile Tutorials: Wasted Effort or Efficiency Boost?* https://www.nngroup.com/articles/mobile-tutorials/

5   Christiano, A., & Neimand, A. (2017). Stop Raising Awareness Already. *Stanford Social Innovation Review*, 15(2), 34–41. https://doi.org/10.48558/7MA6-J918

6   Mertz, Carol [@carolmertz]. (2019). *As I've gotten more into my games studies, I've started noticing a trend with game designers choosing to trim or* [Tweet]. Twitter. https://twitter.com/carolmertz/status/1097526572402262017

7   Burnett, M.M., Stumpf, S., Macbeth, J.C., Makri, S., Beckwith, L., Kwan, I., Peters, A.N., & Jernigan, W. (2016). GenderMag: A Method for Evaluating Software's Gender Inclusiveness. *Interacting with Computers*, 28, 760-787. https://doi.org/10.1093/iwc/iwv046

8   Moreno, Roxana & Mayer, Richard. (2007). Interactive Multimodal Learning Environments. *Educ Psychol Rev*. 19. 309-326. https://www.researchgate.net/publication/227033633_Interactive_Multimodal_Learning_Environments

9   GDC. (2019). *How I Got My Mom to Play Through Plants vs. Zombies* [Video]. YouTube. https://www.youtube.com/watch?v=fbzhHSexzpY

10 Kontra, C., Lyons, D. J., Fischer, S. M., & Beilock, S. L. (2015). Physical Experience Enhances Science Learning. *Psychological Science*, 26(6), 737-749. https://doi.org/10.1177/0956797615569355

Chapter 2 | Getting Ready for New Users

1 Halliday, Josh. (2010). Times loses almost 90% of online readership. *The Guardian*. https://www.theguardian.com/media/2010/jul/20/times-paywall-readership

2 *Solid Customer Onboarding Drives Higher Retention, Willingness to Pay.* (2019). https://www.paddle.com/studios/shows/profitwell-report/positive-onboarding

3 Zuniga, Agustin et al. (2019). Tortoise or Hare? Quantifying the Effects of Performance on Mobile App Retention. *WWW '19: The World Wide Web Conference.* 2517-2528. https://www.researchgate.net/publication/333067690_Tortoise_or_Hare_Quantifying_the_Effects_of_Performance_on_Mobile_App_Retention

4 Chadburn, Matt & Lahav, Gadi. (2016). *A Faster ft.com.* https://medium.com/ft-product-technology/a-faster-ft-com-10e7c077dc1c

5 Coyier, Chris. (2019). The Fight Against Layout Jank. *CSS Tricks.* https://css-tricks.com/the-fight-against-layout-jank/

6 Chahal, Mindi. (2015). Consumers are 'dirtying' databases with false details. *MarketingWeek*. https://www.marketingweek.com/consumers-are-dirtying-databases-with-false-details/

7 Deque Systems. (2019). *New Research Shows How "The Internet is Unavailable" to Blind Users.* https://www.deque.com/blog/research-shows-internet-is-unavailable-to-blind-users

8 Francis, T. & Hoefel, F. (2018). *'True Gen': Generation Z and its implications for companies.* https://www.mckinsey.com/industries/consumer-packaged-goods/our-insights/true-gen-generation-z-and-its-implications-for-companies

9 Sirk, Christopher. Patagonia Customer Base & Rise of Environmental Ethos. *CRM.org*. https://crm.org/articles/patagonias-customer-base-and-the-rise-of-an-environmental-ethos

10 Beer, Jeff. (2018). How Patagonia Grows Every Time It Amplifies Its Social Mission. *Fast Company.* www.fastcompany.com/40525452/how-patagonia-grows-every-time-it-amplifies-its-social-mission

Chapter 3 | Mapping Onboarding Journeys

1 Korman, Jonathan [@miniver]. *If you know the intermediate-use destination, you can strip stuff away to figure out what essentials to reveal for first-time use* [Tweet]. Twitter. https://www.twitter.com/miniver/status/806977351187730432

2   GOV.UK Design Community. (2019). *Getting the scope of your trans-action right.* https://www.gov.uk/service-manual/design/scoping-your-service#only-put-information-inside-a-service-if-it-needs-to-be-there

3   Mixpanel Team. (2018). *Magic numbers are an illusion.* https://mixpanel.com/blog/magic-numbers-are-an-illusion

Chapter 4 | Guidance In Action

1   Spool, Jared. (2009). *The $300 Million Button.* https://articles.centercentre.com/three_hund_million_button

2   Keith, Jeremy. (2020). *Saving Forms.* https://adactio.com/journal/17516

3   Tugend, Alina. (2012). Praise Is Fleeting, but Brickbats We Recall. *New York Times.* https://www.nytimes.com/2012/03/24/your-money/why-people-remember-negative-events-more-than-positive-ones.html

4   Murre, J. M., & Dros, J. (2015). Replication and Analysis of Ebbinghaus' Forgetting Curve. *PloS one, 10(7)*, e0120644. https://doi.org/10.1371/journal.pone.0120644

5   Kang, S. H. K. (2016). Spaced Repetition Promotes Efficient and Effective Learning: Policy Implications for Instruction. *Policy Insights from the Behavioral and Brain Sciences*, 3(1), 12-19. https://doi.org/10.1177/2372732215624708

Chapter 5 | Presenting Guidance

1   Fallows, James. (2008). "Clippy" update – now, with organizational anthropology! The Atlantic. https://www.theatlantic.com/technology/archive/2008/04/-quot-clippy-quot-update-now-with-organizational-anthropology/8006

2   (2008). *Affordances and Design.* https://jnd.org/affordances-and-design

3   McCracken, Harry. (2010). *The Bob Chronicles.* https://www.technologizer.com/2010/03/29/microsoft-bob/

4   Spool, Jared. (2011). *Do Users Change Their Settings?* https://archive.uie.com/brainsparks/2011/09/14/do-users-change-their-settings/

5   Pernice, Kara. (2018). *Banner Blindness Revisited: Users Dodge Ads on Mobile and Desktop.* https://www.nngroup.com/articles/banner-blindness-old-and-new-findings/

6   Jenkins, J. et al. (2016). More Harm Than Good? How Messages That Interrupt Can Make Us Vulnerable. Information Systems Research. 27(4):880-896. https://doi.org/10.1287/isre.2016.0644

Chapter 6 | Scaling Guidance

1   GOV.UK Design System. *Patterns.* https://design-system.service.gov.uk/patterns

2   Sedley, A., & Müller, H. (2013). Minimizing change aversion for the google drive launch. *CHI'13 Extended Abstracts on Human Factors in Computing Systems* (pp. 2351-2354). https://research.google/pubs/minimizing-change-aversion-for-the-google-drive-launch

INDEX

notifications 104

Rosson, Mary Beth 10

O

offering alternatives 66–67
onboarding (definition) 8–10
overlays 94–97

P

paradox of the active user 10
performance and reliability 28–29
personalization 114
playthrough content 88
playthrough tutorial 88
presets 86
prioritizing actions 49
product design 80–86
prompts 54–60

R

re-boarding lapsed users 118
reinforcing guidance 76–77
repeatable actions 74–76

S

scoping actions 47–48
setup wizards 100
signup walls 29
siloed onboarding 111–113
Simon, Herbert A. 11
Smith, Jared 12
spaced repetition 76
Spool, Jared 57
support in context 61–63

T

text messages 104

U

unsupported immersion 13–14

V

vanity metrics 20

COLOPHON

The text is set in Source Serif 4, an open source typeface designed by Frank Grießhammer, and Jost, designed by Owen Earl from indestructible type. Headlines are set in Sofia Sans Extra Condensed from Lettersoup, Botio Nikoltchev, and Ani Petrova. Cover & chapter titles are set in Morganite by Rajesh Rajput.

ABOUT THE AUTHOR

Krystal Higgins is a UX designer who connects the dots between products, systems, and the people who use them. She's taught teams across the world how to design better, human-centered onboarding at events like SXSW, An Event Apart, UX London, and UX Days Tokyo; through her catalog of first-run experiences at first-run-ux.com; and through her onboarding articles at kryshiggins.com. Krystal has more than 15 years of experience designing innovative products for mobile, web, wearable, and new platforms at companies like NVIDIA, eBay, and Google. When she's not working on tech-meets-humans projects, she enjoys painting, illustration, and scuba diving.

www.ingramcontent.com/pod-product-compliance
Ingram Content Group UK Ltd.
Pitfield, Milton Keynes, MK11 3LW, UK
UKHW051521020225
4411UKWH00026B/232

9 781763 673403